Journal of Desires

Journal of Desires

A Daily Diary with
Readings and Reflections
Guiding You
to Fulfillment of
Your Lifelong Wishes
and Dreams

LAUREL VUKOVIĆ

Library of Congress Cataloging-in-Publication Data

Vukovic, Laurel.
    Journal of desires : a daily diary with readings and reflections guiding you to fulfillment of your lifelong wishes and dreams / Laurel Vukovic.
    p. cm.
    ISBN 0-7352-0237-0 (pbk.)
    1. Conduct of life—Quotations, maxims, etc. 2. Diaries, Authorship. I. Title.

BF637.C5 V85 2001
158.1—dc21
                                                                    00-045651

Acquisitions Editor: Ed Claflin
Production Editor: Mariann Hutlak
Composition: Amy Koval
Interior Design: Suzanne Behnke

©2001 by Prentice Hall Press

All rights reserved. No part of this book may be reproduced, in any form or by any means, without permission in writing from the publisher.

Printed in the United States of America

10 9 8 7 6 5 4 3 2 1

ISBN 0-7352-0237-0

ATTENTION: CORPORATIONS AND SCHOOLS

Prentice Hall Press books are available at quantity discounts with bulk purchase for educational, business, or sales promotional use. For information, please write to: Prentice Hall Direct/Special Sales, 240 Frisch Court, Paramus, New Jersey 07652. Please supply: title of book, ISBN, quantity, how the book will be used, date needed.

 Paramus, NJ 07652

http://www.phdirect.com

Dedication

I dedicate this book to your authentic self.

May your beautiful and unique spirit shine brightly
and illuminate your life.

Contents

Introduction xvii

Week 1
Discovering Your Life's Purpose 1

Week 2
Living by Your Own Light 7

Week 3
Trusting Your Intuition 13

Week 4
Taking Time for Solitude 19

Week 5
Living in the Moment 25

Week 6
Letting Go of the Past 31

Week 7
The Healing Balm of Forgiveness 37

Week 8
Learning to Love Yourself 43

Week 9
Building Self-Confidence 49

Week 10
Finding Courage 55

Week 11
Strengthening Hope 61

Week 12
Saying "Thank You" to Life 67

Week 13
Creating Happiness 73

Week 14
    Rekindling Enthusiasm 79

Week 15
    Recapturing a Sense of Wonder 85

Week 16
    Taking Risks 91

Week 17
    Nourishing Your Dreams 97

Week 18
    Accessing the Power of Action 103

Week 19
    Finding Support for Your Dreams 109

Week 20
    Recognizing Opportunity 115

Week 21
    Defining Success 121

Week 22
    Keeping the Faith 127

Week 23
    Flowing with Change 133

Week 24
    Taking One Day at a Time 139

Week 25
    Cultivating Simplicity 145

Week 26
    The Joy of Learning 151

Week 27
    Finding Your Life's Work 157

Week 28
    Remembering How to Play 163

Week 29
    Seeking Adventure 169

Week 30
    Making Time for Pleasure 175

Week 31
    Embracing Your Sensuality 181

Week 32
    The Art of Seeing 187

Week 33
    Attuning to Sound 193

Week 34
    The Delights of Fragrance 199

Week 35
    The Healing Pleasure of Touch 205

Week 36
    Nourishment for the Body and Soul 211

Week 37
    Appreciating Beauty 217

Week 38
 Reconnecting with Nature 223

Week 39
 Living Abundantly 229

Week 40
 Engaging Your Imagination 235

Week 41
 Rediscovering Your Creativity 241

Week 42
 Finding Humor in Life 247

Week 43
 The Art of Contentment 253

Week 44
 Nurturing the Heart of Compassion 259

Week 45
 The Spirit of Generosity 265

Week 46
　　Connecting with Friends 271

Week 47
　　Rediscovering Love 277

Week 48
　　The Sanctuary of Home 283

Week 49
　　Enjoying Optimal Health 289

Week 50
　　The Restorative Power of Relaxation 295

Week 51
　　Cultivating Peace 301

Week 52
　　The Essence of Spirituality 307

　　About the Author   313

Acknowledgements

Being given the opportunity to write this book was a dream come true, and proof once again that the urgings of my authentic self lead to miraculous happenings. For more than two decades I have kept a journal, and my daily writings have provided the seeds for the weekly reflections that you will find in these pages. Along the way, I have been inspired by writers whom I consider to be kindred souls on the same path, including Julia Cameron, Barbara Sher, Shakti Gawain, Sarah Ban Breathnach, Thomas Moore, Jon Kabat-Zinn, and M.J. Ryan, among others. I am also appreciative of the collective wisdom of the many people whom I have quoted in this book, and to John Cook, for his excellent reference, The Book of Positive Quotations.

I was fortunate to be born into a family that values living life to the fullest, and am grateful to my mother and father for encouraging a sense of wonder, appreciation, and enthusiasm for life. I have also been blessed with many friends who share the desire to live an authentic life, and they continue to be a source of loving support. I am especially grateful to Pat Righter for her wise presence in my life.

My deepest appreciation goes to Ed Claflin, my editor at Prentice Hall Direct, who conceived of *The Journal of Desires* and has been wonderfully positive and encouraging throughout the writing process. My thanks also to Angela Miller for helping us connect, and to Mariann Hutlak for her attention to detail in bringing this book into print.

And finally, my love and gratitude to Eric and Amanda, for their love and support.

Introduction

Desires are not frivolous things. On the contrary, they are the urgings of your soul. You can discover the life you are meant to live by listening carefully to them. The most accurate guide for living a rich and satisfying life lies within you. By following your desires, you will be led to the core of your authentic self.

Some people fear that following their desires will lead them into a life of selfishness and reckless abandon. That would be a risk if you were indulging fear-based desires such as the inappropriate use of alcohol, drugs, food, sex, shopping, or the many other ways we use to escape from life instead of embracing it. Through this journal, however, I am encouraging you to pursue the desires that arise from your *authentic self*, which is always looking out for your highest good.

True desires are the language of the heart and soul. They are not meant to be ignored or suppressed—in fact, to do so invites emotional and spiritual pain. A sense of emptiness, depression, questions about the meaning of one's life, and discouragement all point to a loss of connection with the authentic self, the soul of one's being. Honor your desires, and they will help you find the way home to yourself.

I offer you in this book fifty-two topics to contemplate week-by-week throughout the year, that weave together the sensory and the spiritual, the material and the esoteric. The topics range from finding solitude and letting go of the past to building self-confidence, learning to play, and delighting in the sensory pleasures of sights, smells, tastes, touch, and sounds. As you read through and reflect on these various topics day by day, you will be awakening to and reconnecting with your heart's desires, and will have the opportunity to explore taking steps to bring your desires into reality. Some of the steps are practical, and others are focused more on inward exploration, but all are meant to help you discover your authentic self.

Discovering and living your authentic life is a lifelong process of inquiry, exploration, and trial and error. This journal is meant to be a companion in your exploration, and offers an opportunity to reflect, to meditate, and to hear the voice of your inner wisdom. If you do only this, I assure you that your life will be transformed. You will discover insights and truths about yourself, half-forgotten dreams, and the desires of your authentic self. I wish you joy in your journey.

Laurel Vukovic

Journal of Desires

Discovering Your Life's Purpose

My friend Joanie recently commented that she wasn't really certain of what she wanted in life. Anyone looking at her from the outside would judge her to be a successful woman—she has a loving family, a successful career, and a beautiful home. She's grateful for all that she has, but she wakes up every morning with the feeling that something important is missing from her life.

I know a lot of people who suffer from the same sense of incompleteness. I've felt it, too, and more than once in my life. I've learned to honor the feelings of "something's missing" as messages from my authentic self, and I've found that exploring those messages—instead of ignoring them—invariably leads me back to the path of my life's purpose.

In her inspiring book *Wishcraft: How to Get What You Really Want*, Barbara Sher writes, "If you are low in energy, if you need a lot of sleep and feel like you're always dragging yourself around at half throttle, it may not be because you need vitamins or have low blood sugar. It may be because you have not found your purpose in life."

We each have a unique purpose in life. Actually, most of us have more than one. Your life purpose will more than likely evolve and change over time, and it may have little to do with what you are doing now—even if you are very successful.

So how do you know if you are following your true life path?

The test is simple. Does your life fill you with joy? Do you look forward to each day? This doesn't mean that you won't ever feel uncertain, or that you won't experience emotional ups and downs. But most of the time, do you feel a passionate interest in your life?

If you don't, then it's time to reconnect with the dreams of your authentic self. To live your life's purpose, you must rediscover what you love *now*.

Barbara Sher suggests an exercise that I've found immensely helpful. I use it every few years, especially at those times when I have the nagging feeling that "something's missing." Imagine that you have five lives to live—lives in which you could fully explore a lifestyle, talent, or interest that you have. What would you do in each life? Where and how would you live?

Imagine your five lives in rich detail, and journal about them if you choose. These imaginings offer valuable insights into your life's purpose, and the more you bring them into reality, the happier and more fulfilled you will be. For example, if you dream of being an artist, you might enroll in a painting class. If you long to live in the country and live off the land, you might plant a vegetable garden and learn to make jams and pickles. Do you harbor a secret desire to be an anthropologist? Perhaps you could volunteer to be a docent at a museum.

As you explore each of your five lives, think of ways that you can bring aspects of these desires into your daily life.

SUNDAY

Follow your bliss. Find where it is and don't be afraid to follow it.

—Joseph Campbell

MONDAY

Destiny is not a matter of chance, it is a matter of choice;
it is not a thing to be waited for, it is a thing to be achieved.

—William Jennings Bryan

Tuesday

You will recognize your own path when you come upon it, because you will suddenly have all the energy and imagination you will ever need.

—Barbara Sher

Wednesday

The aim of life is self-development, to realize one's nature perfectly.

—Oscar Wilde

THURSDAY

*We all live with the objective of being happy;
our lives are all different, and yet the same.*

—Anne Frank

FRIDAY

*To be nobody—but yourself—in a world which is doing its best, night and day,
to make you everybody else—means to fight the hardest battle which
any human being can fight, and never stop fighting.*

—E. E. Cummings

Saturday

Any path is only a path, and there is no affront, to oneself or to others, in dropping it if that is what your heart tells you.

—Carlos Castaneda

Week 2

Living by Your Own Light

Knowing what you love and living according to your heart's desires and the urgings of your soul is the quickest path to living your authentic life. It is also a challenging path, because we want to be accepted—and in doing so, we often forfeit our true desires.

It's an insidious process. You might not even realize how much of yourself you have sublimated, and how much you have suppressed the voice of your authentic self. The suppression begins in childhood, when we accept the desires of another as more important than our own. We want to please, we don't want to disappoint another, and so we compromise, acquiesce, tell ourselves it really doesn't matter anyway.

Sometimes it *doesn't* matter. Compromise is what allows for harmony, and it's not realistic or generous to always insist upon your own way. Neither is it healthy, however, to continually put yourself second, to deny your needs, and to compromise to the point of not even knowing anymore who you truly are.

Your authentic self speaks clearly to you through desires and preferences. Acknowledging and honoring your wishes and penchants strengthens your authentic self, and helps you to fully become the unique individual that you are. You have gifts to offer to the world that no one else can provide, and the only way you can bring these gifts to fruition is to nurture the unique individual that you are.

This week, reflect upon the uniqueness of your being. What do you love? What inspires you and makes you glad to be alive? Examine your life in detail, and notice your preferences in all that you do. Don't be surprised if you feel uncertainties arise.

You may find it difficult to know what you want or like if you have spent many years suppressing your authentic self in favor of pleasing others. Start small, and have fun with the process of rediscovering your preferences.

What colors make you feel good? What type of music do you like? What are your favorite foods, movies, and books? As you become more comfortable expressing your preferences, expand your repertoire to your work, your relationships, your leisure time, your spiritual practice—to all areas of your life.

The more you express your unique preferences, the more honestly you will be living. It's another way of coming home to your authentic self.

Thursday

*I'll walk where my own nature would be leading;
it vexes me to choose another guide.*

—Emily Brontë

Friday

We will discover the nature of our particular genius when we stop trying to conform to our own or to other people's models, learn to be ourselves, and allow our natural channel to open.

—Shakti Gawain

Saturday

This above all: to thine own self be true.

—William Shakespeare

Week 3

Trusting Your Intuition

Following the guidance of your intuition is one of the most powerful steps you can take to reconnect with your authentic self. Intuition speaks to us in different ways: Some hear it clearly as a voice. More often, though, the wisdom within you communicates through dreams, feelings, and an inexplicable sense of knowing what you should do in any given moment.

Intuition can all too easily be dismissed because it is rarely based on logic or intellect. But each time you turn away from your inner wisdom, you take a step away from your authentic self.

It's not always easy to discern the voice of intuition. Years of living according to external "shoulds" can cloud intuition, and fear makes it difficult to trust your inner voice. To recover your connection to your intuition, you must learn to trust yourself again. You must be willing to risk, to make mistakes, and to be gentle with yourself in the process.

The rewards of reestablishing a strong bond with your inner wisdom are great. As you follow the guidance of your intuition, you will have a clear sense of purpose in life, and you will be more attuned to the opportunities that surround you.

You can reconnect with your inner wisdom by creating an inner space of trust and openness. It's often easiest to access your intuition when your body and mind are relaxed, perhaps during the early morning hours, before the activities of the day occupy your mind.

Don't despair if it seems as though you can't distinguish your intuition from all of the other voices that fill your head with chatter. It takes time and trust to rebuild a relationship with your inner wisdom. Know, however, that the more you follow your internal guidance, the stronger and clearer your intuition will become.

This week, consider how much you rely on your intuition. How does your inner wisdom communicate with you? Have there been times when you have relied on your intuition for making decisions? Is your intuition a trusted guide in your life's journey?

Journaling is a wonderful process for dialoguing with your inner wisdom. Ask a question in writing, and then write freely for 15 or 20 minutes in a relaxed way without censoring what you are writing.

How do you know when you have connected with your inner wisdom? If you feel renewed energy and a sense of clarity about the next step to take, you are surely connected with your intuition.

Sunday

We each need to let our intuition guide us, and then be willing to follow that guidance directly and fearlessly.

—Shakti Gawain

Monday

Spend time every day listening to what your muse is trying to tell you.

—Saint Bartholomew

TUESDAY

If you do not express your own original ideas, if you do not listen to your own being, you will have betrayed yourself.

—Rollo May

WEDNESDAY

Trust the instinct to the end, though you can render no reason.

—Ralph Waldo Emerson

Week 4

Taking Time for Solitude

For years, I've set aside an hour first thing every weekday morning to journal, meditate, and reflect on the day ahead. Day in and day out, this is the common thread that weaves through my life and brings peace and a sense of purpose to my days.

I have the luxury of this solitary time during the week, but on the weekends, when my family is at home in the mornings, I don't find it so easy to take time for solitude. Somehow, it's just not the same with other people wandering through the house, and I feel the need to make breakfast or otherwise interact.

I notice a definite difference in how the day unfolds when I first take time for solitude. I feel centered, more connected with my authentic self, and happier. Therefore, I've recently begun to take time for myself on weekend mornings—and surprisingly, I've found that everyone is just fine on their own for that brief hour. I've realized that solitude is a gift that I must give to myself.

Time spent in solitude helps us to reconnect with the deepest recesses of our authentic selves. Time alone gives our souls breathing space. When our minds and bodies are not occupied with the daily round of life activities that normally fill our days to overflowing, there is time to rediscover who we are and to maintain the connection with what is most important to us.

To reap the greatest benefits, make solitude an established part of your daily life. You may choose to spend your time journaling, meditating, dreaming, or creating. Think of solitude as a vacation for your soul. It's a respite from the daily demands of life that can all too easily drown out the voice of your authentic self. A vacation in Hawaii or the Caribbean is great, but the most deeply renewing place that you can go to on a regular basis is within yourself.

This week, reflect on how much time you give yourself for solitude. When did you last have time to yourself? How do you feel about taking time for yourself? What might you do with an hour of solitude each day? How might you create that time for yourself?

THURSDAY

Learn to get in touch with the silence within yourself and know that everything in this life has a purpose.

—Elisabeth Kubler-Ross, M.D.

FRIDAY

There is only one journey. Going inside yourself.

—Ranier Maria Rilke

Saturday

Inside myself is a place where I live all alone and that's where you renew your springs that never dry up.

–Pearl S. Buck

Week 5

Living in the Moment

I recently returned from my daily morning walk, and as I walked through the front door, realized that I had no conscious awareness of where I had been or what I had seen. While my feet were carrying me along my accustomed path, my mind was busy going over my schedule for the day, planning dinner, and ruminating about a work problem. Instead of feeling refreshed and energized as I usually do following a walk, I felt tense, and as though I had wasted a precious hour of my life. The following morning, I approached my walk with the intention of being conscious in the moment. I felt the cool morning breeze on my skin and smelled the fragrant pines and herbs along the path. I stopped to watch a great blue heron fishing in a pond, and delighted in the masses of wildflowers blooming in the hills. I returned from this walk feeling peaceful, happy, and grateful for all that I had experienced.

Learning to be present in the moment is one of the greatest gifts you can give to yourself. But most of us spend the majority of our time either in the past or the future. We ruminate about the past, lamenting what could have been or regretting paths not taken. Or we worry about the future, imagining all sorts of anxiety-provoking scenarios. Even focusing too much on what's next on the list of "things to do" takes attention away from the present moment. Every time you mentally step away from the present, you turn your back on life. The only time that exists is this moment, right now. Reflecting on the past offers you the wisdom of experience, but that wisdom can only be used in the present. As for the future, it has meaning only when it becomes the present moment. The most powerful action you can take to ensure a satisfying future is to live your life to the fullest *today*.

This week, observe how present you are in your daily life. How much time do you spend in the past or the future? How often are you truly awake in the present moment? Simply notice, without judging. You might try taking a walk outdoors, paying attention in a relaxed way to all that surrounds you. Every time your mind wanders to the past or jumps ahead to the future, gently bring your focus back to the present moment. How do you feel when you pay attention in this way? How might you bring more present-moment awareness into your life?

Sunday

Only that day dawns to which we are awake.

—Henry David Thoreau

Monday

Every second is of infinite value.

—Johann Wolfgang von Goethe

Tuesday

To finish the moment, to find the journey's end in every step of the road, to live the greatest number of good hours, is wisdom.

--Ralph Waldo Emerson

Wednesday

Life is not lost by dying; life is lost minute by minute, day by day, in all the thousand small, uncaring ways.

--Stephen Saint Vincent Benet

THURSDAY

I live now and only now, and I will do what I want to do this moment and not what I decided was best for me yesterday.

--Hugh Prather

FRIDAY

Life is all memory except for the one present moment that goes by so quick you can hardly catch it going.

--Tennessee Williams

SATURDAY

The passing moment is all we can be sure of;
it is only common sense to extract its utmost value from it.

—William Somerset Maugham

Letting Go of the Past

Reminiscing about the past can be a wonderful remembrance of people, places, and events. For too many of us, though, the past is heavily weighted with memories of things that we wish we had done differently, mistakes we berate ourselves for making, and paths we wish we had taken or not taken.

It's true that we learn from our past experiences. But if we continue to live in the past, all of our energy can be consumed by replaying over and over the mistakes we have made, regrets we carry, and pain we've suffered.

Focusing on the past prevents us from living fully in the present moment. We all have regrets. There are many things I can think of that I would do differently if I had the opportunity to live my life over again. But the truth is that without the benefit of hindsight, I would likely make the same choices that I made before. It is only through experience that we learn and grow, and this learning is one of the great gifts the past has to offer.

We are all, in every moment, doing the best we can do. This doesn't mean we aren't capable of improvement, or in another situation we couldn't do better. It's important to recognize that many factors, both external and internal, converge to determine the choices we make and the actions we take. Why not give ourselves the benefit of compassion, and trust that we have done the best we could do at the time?

The past can be a valuable teacher. By reflecting on the past without self-recrimination, you'll enable yourself to make the best possible choices today. When you find yourself mulling over the past, try shifting your awareness to that of an interested and compassionate observer. Trust that you were doing the best you could do at the time, and know that living well today is your best assurance of creating not only a satisfying present, but also a past of happy memories.

This week, reflect on the wisdom you have gained through your life experiences. What can you use to chart your course for a satisfying life now?

Sunday

Life can only be understood backwards, but it must be lived forward.

—Søren Kierkegaard

Monday

Let the past drift away with the water.

—Japanese saying

Tuesday

No longer forward nor behind I look in hope or fear;
But, grateful, take the good I find, The best of now and here.

—John Greenleaf Whittier

Wednesday

The first recipe for happiness is: Avoid too lengthy meditations on the past.

—Andre Maurois

THURSDAY

Forgiveness means letting go of the past.

—Gerald Jampolsky

FRIDAY

The only thing I regret about my past is the length of it. If I had to live my life again, I'd make the same mistakes, only sooner.

—Tallulah Bankhead

Saturday

> Look not mournfully into the past, it comes not back again.
> Wisely improve the present, it is thine.
>
> –Henry Wadsworth Longfellow

Week 7

The Healing Balm of Forgiveness

More than twenty years ago, I read a small book called *Love is Letting Go of Fear* that significantly changed the way I viewed the world. In this simple book, author Gerald Jampolsky, a psychiatrist, proposed that all of us, at all times, are acting either from love or from fear. He explained that anger, greed, dishonesty, selfishness—indeed, all of the behaviors that cause so much suffering—are rooted in fear. I was struck by this assertion, and began to examine my own behavior and the behavior of others around me.

As I looked closely, I saw that unpleasant, unkind, and even aggressive behaviors masked fears of intimacy, fears of not having enough, and fears of inadequacy. I felt enormous compassion for others, and for myself with this realization.

When I forget this—and I do—I notice how easy it is to become angry and to nurse resentments. I'm not saying that anger is an inappropriate emotion. It's often a cue from your authentic self that you have somehow been violated—or that you have betrayed yourself. If you take action to take care of yourself and stop giving your power away to others, your anger will dissipate.

Resentments are a different story. They smolder within, erode your well-being, and keep you in a victim's role.

Most of us have a storehouse of resentments, from ancient childhood wounds to yesterday's anger at a spouse or co-worker. Acknowl-edging your resentments is the first step toward letting them go.

Take a moment to reflect on the resentments you are holding. How do you feel as you review them? Probably not very peaceful, nor very happy. Resentments erode peace of mind like a splinter that festers under the skin.

Even with the pain caused by resentments, forgiveness is not an easy task, however, and it usually doesn't work to simply decide to be forgiving. That's because forgiveness arises not only from making the decision to forgive, but from true understanding and compassion.

Take time this week to go within, and reflect on the resentments you are carrying. You might find it helpful to make a list of everyone you feel has hurt you, describing in detail the event and your feelings. As you do this, see if you can recognize the role fear played in their actions and also in your response.

Write a letter to each person (you don't have to mail it) telling him or her how you feel and stating clearly how you will take care of yourself in the future. Don't rush the process, but take action to heal your resentments by bringing them into the light of awareness and compassion.

Sunday

The practice of forgiveness is our most important
contribution to the healing of the world.

—Marianne Williamson

Monday

I can have peace of mind only when I forgive rather than judge.

—Gerald Jampolsky

Tuesday

Forgiveness is made easy when we can identify with others and admit to our own imperfections and an equal capacity for wrongdoing.

—Leo Buscaglia

Wednesday

All feelings, beliefs, and emotional patterns must be brought to the light of consciousness in order to be dissolved. When the light shines into the darkness, the darkness disappears.

—Shakti Gawain

Thursday

Forgiveness is the answer to the child's dream of a miracle by which what is broken is made whole again, what is soiled is again made clean.

—Dag Hammarskjöld

Friday

How unhappy is he who cannot forgive himself.

—Publilius Syrus

Saturday

Those who are free of resentful thoughts surely find peace.

—Buddha

Week 8

Learning to Love Yourself

Comparing ourselves with others, or even to an internal standard of how we think we should be, is one of the most demoralizing acts we can take against our authentic selves. In contrast, learning to accept and love ourselves as we are right now and appreciating our uniqueness is a great step toward freeing ourselves to become all that we can be.

"We tend to think being hard on ourselves will make us strong. But it is cherishing ourselves that gives us strength," writes Julia Cameron in her wonderful book *The Artist's Way*.

Learning to cherish oneself is often a lifelong task, but it is perhaps the most important work of your life. Just as a child blossoms with love and acceptance, so does the inner child that resides within each of us.

Most of us have difficulties truly appreciating ourselves. We live in a society obsessed with self-improvement, and while there are certainly benefits to be had from improving oneself, there is also the implicit message that you aren't good enough just as you are. Under the guise of improving ourselves, we are constantly examining every aspect of our beings with a critical eye.

Self-improvement can easily tilt into a quest for perfection, and perfection by its very nature is a losing proposition because it is always just out of reach.

We each have an inner critic, and making peace with this part of yourself will help to release you from the prison of perfectionism and self-judgment. In their enlightening book *Embracing Your Inner Critic*, Hal and Sidra Stone explain that the motivation of the inner critic is to make us acceptable and to keep us from getting hurt.

Recognizing that your inner critic is concerned with your well-being can help you to form a healthier relationship with this part of yourself. When you understand the underlying fear of the inner critic, you defuse its power and are on the way to freeing yourself from its tyranny.

This week, reflect on your relationship with your inner critic. Are you aware of the voice within you that criticizes you? You might find it helpful to communicate with your inner critic through journaling, asking it what it is afraid of. How might you reassure your inner critic that you can take care of yourself? How might you cherish the unique being that you are?

Sunday

Because you are like no other being ever created since the beginning of time, you are incomparable.

—Brenda Ueland

Monday

There is a proper balance between not asking enough of oneself and asking or expecting too much.

—May Sarton

Tuesday

No one can make you feel inferior without your consent.

—Eleanor Roosevelt

Wednesday

As soon as you trust yourself, you will know how to live.

—Johann Wolfgang von Goethe

THURSDAY

I exist as I am, that is enough, If no other in the world be aware, I sit content, And if each and all be aware, I sit content.

—Walt Whitman

FRIDAY

Perfectionism is not a quest for the best. It is a pursuit of the worst in ourselves, the part that tells us that nothing we do will ever be good enough—that we should try again.

—Julia Cameron

SATURDAY

We expect more of ourselves than we have any right to.

—Oliver Wendell Holmes, Jr.

Building Self-Confidence

We were all born with a healthy amount of self-confidence—the confidence it takes to learn how to walk, to talk, to master the most basic skills of life. But few of us as adults possess the same self-confidence we had as children. Somewhere along the way, we lost trust in ourselves.

If you feel you lack self-confidence, the origins were likely in your childhood, when parents, teachers, or other authority figures tried to protect you from the "realities of life" by helping you take your dreams down a notch or two. Know that a lack of self-confidence is based in fear—the fear of not being able to do something, the fear of not being good enough, the fear of being judged by others.

Self-confidence means believing that we are capable of doing what we want to do. It means believing that we have the resilience to pick ourselves up and try again if we fail the first time—or even the first 100 times.

Self-confidence is essential for allowing your authentic self to fully emerge. As you begin to rediscover your core desires, you will undoubtedly find many bits and pieces of yourself that have long been neglected. These buried dreams are the artifacts of your authentic self, and dusting them off and reconsidering them can help you piece together a life that is a magnificent, one-of-a-kind creation—yours, and yours alone.

This week, consider whether a lack of confidence has stopped you from pursuing a heartfelt desire or dream. Can you recall any messages given to you as a child that planted seeds of lack of self-trust? Have you had experiences that have made you afraid to try something you are secretly longing to attempt? How would your life be different if you embodied self-confidence?

Consider experimenting with something you would like to try. Instead of making the goal your primary focus, however, concentrate on enjoying the journey. Give yourself permission, from the beginning, to make lots of mistakes. Be again as a child, self-confidently exploring your place in the world.

SUNDAY

As soon as you trust yourself, you will know how to live.

—Johann Wolfgang von Goethe

MONDAY

Our doubts are traitors, and make us lose the good we oft might win, by fearing to attempt.

—William Shakespeare

Tuesday

Self-trust is the first secret of success.

—Ralph Waldo Emerson

Wednesday

If one advances confidently in the direction of his dreams, and endeavors to live the life which he has imagined, he will meet with a success unexpected in common hours.

—Henry David Thoreau

Thursday

It is not because things are difficult that we do not dare; it is because we do not dare that they are difficult.

—Seneca

Friday

Faith in oneself is the best and safest course.

—Michelangelo

SATURDAY

Shoot for the moon. Even if you miss it you will land among the stars.
—Les Brown

Finding Courage

We often ascribe courage to those who perform outstanding acts of bravery—those who save children from burning buildings or rescue lost hikers in blinding blizzards. Yet, courage is not reserved for those few who are awarded medals for their heroism. It takes enormous courage to live consciously, to cultivate awareness, and to be willing to express your authentic self.

Consider how many things you have postponed or avoided because you were concerned about someone else criticizing or disapproving of you. I'm not referring to illegal or immoral activities, but the desires of your soul that you have ignored because you feared rejection.

How many times have you said *no* to something when you really wanted to say *yes*? What secret desires have you kept hidden away because you were afraid of failure? This happens to all of us.

The fear of living fully takes root in childhood, when we first encounter the judgments of others. Wanting to please, we begin to censor ourselves so that we will gain approval. We internalize the judgments we hear, and often become far harsher critics of ourselves than others could ever be.

Life becomes painfully narrow when you limit yourself to the parameters of what your inner judge deems it safe for you to express. Thus, your authentic self goes underground and languishes from lack of expression. This is where cultivating courage serves you well.

We are all called upon to be courageous at various times in life. It takes courage to face relationship difficulties, financial problems, serious illness, and death. That courage will be there when you need it. It's the courage to live authentically on a daily basis that needs to be nourished.

This week, reflect on your buried dreams and desires, the hidden secrets that your authentic self is longing to express. Don't be surprised if you feel uncertain. The inner judge can be so strong that it often suppresses even the longings of your inner self. Try asking, "How would I live if no one else was watching? What would I do if I wasn't afraid of doing it badly?" Listen with compassion, and be aware of any feelings, images, and thoughts that arise.

Sunday

Life shrinks or expands in proportion to one's courage.

--Anaïs Nin

Monday

Life only demands from you the strength you possess.

--Dag Hammarskjöld

Tuesday

The human spirit is stronger than anything that can happen to it.

—George C. Scott

Wednesday

*We have what we seek. It is there all the time,
and if we give it time, it will make itself known to us.*

—Thomas Merton

Thursday

Start by doing what's necessary, then what's possible, and suddenly you are doing the impossible.

--Saint Francis of Assisi

Friday

Courage is the price that life exacts for granting peace, the soul that knows it not, knows no release from little things.

--Amelia Earhart

Saturday

It is our light, not our darkness, that most frightens us.
We ask ourselves, who am I to be brilliant, gorgeous, talented, and fabulous?
Actually, who are you not to be?

—Nelson Mandela

Strengthening Hope

A life without hope would be a difficult and painful life, for it would be a life devoid of possibilities, a life without opportunities for growth and change. To live without hope is to merely exist, and to not really live at all.

Yet, many people fear to hope, and refuse to "get their hopes up." Perhaps you have been given that exact message by your parents, teachers, friends, or business associates. Their thinking seems logical—if you don't have hopes, then you can't be disappointed. What a terribly barren way to live!

Hope arises from the core of the authentic self. It inspires us to try new experiences, to stretch and grow. It is also the balm that soothes the inevitable bumps and bruises of life and encourages us to get up and try again. Life becomes narrow and small without hope. Fear rules, and dullness prevails.

A life filled with hope, on the other hand, is a life of inspiration, encouragement, passion, and creative risk-taking. Hope sustains courage when life presents obstacles, and sometimes it is the only light we have to follow when life becomes painfully challenging.

This week, reflect on your feelings about hope. What kind of messages did you get about hope when you were growing up? Consider whether you were encouraged to reach for the stars, or whether you came from a family that was fearful of hoping for too much lest they be disappointed. What are the secret hopes of your heart, your spirit, your authentic self?

SUNDAY

Hope is the thing with feathers that perches in the soul and sings the tune without words and never stops at all.

--EMILY DICKINSON

MONDAY

Optimism is the faith that leads to achievement. Nothing can be done without hope or confidence.

--HELEN KELLER

Tuesday

Hope is an adventure, a going forward, a confident search for a rewarding life.

–Karl Menninger, M.D.

Wednesday

In the face of uncertainty, there is nothing wrong with hope.

–O. Carl Simonton, M.D.

THURSDAY

In the midst of winter, I found within me an invincible summer.

—ALBERT CAMUS

FRIDAY

It's never too late—in fiction or in life—to revise.

—NANCY THAYER

Saturday

We should not let our fears hold us back from pursuing our hopes.

—John F. Kennedy

Week 12

Saying "Thank You" to Life

Most of us remember to say "thank you" when we receive a birthday or holiday gift. We're aware that failing to express appreciation would be thought inconsiderate and ungrateful. Yet, how often do you remember to give thanks for the daily gifts that life offers to you? A beautiful sunrise, a cup of tea, a hot shower, a hug from a loved one...and all this in just the first half hour of the day. How much we take for granted!

I have come to believe that, above all else, practicing gratitude is essential for happiness. If you're not grateful for all that you have in this moment, you will never feel you have enough—you will always see your cup as half empty. To practice gratitude means awakening to the truth that your cup may be half empty, but it is also half full.

It's impossible to feel lasting joy or serenity without gratitude because the mind is continually searching for the next pleasure, acquisition, or accomplishment. There is no end to wanting, and the constant striving for more, bigger, and better leads to frustration, crankiness, and a prevailing sense of emptiness. When you practice gratitude, however, you are preparing your heart and spirit for the experience of joy.

Gratitude is also a powerful tool for self-transformation. The simple act of giving thanks for the blessings of your daily life awakens you to all you have now, and opens you fully to the opportunities that surround you.

This week, take a moment to remember a time when you felt profoundly grateful. You might want to write about that event in detail, and be aware of the feelings that fill your heart now as you recall that situation. Consider making a list, each day, of ten things that happened during the day for which you are grateful. This can be a life-changing practice, because it teaches you to look for the small blessings in life and to fully appreciate all that you have now.

Learning to be grateful is not easy, but neither is it difficult. It simply takes practice, and a willingness to look for what is right about our lives instead of what is wrong.

Sunday

If the only prayer you say in your whole life is "thank you," that would suffice.

—Meister Eckhart

Monday

Just to be is a blessing. Just to live is holy.

—Rabbi Abraham Heschel

Tuesday

I have learned, in whatsoever state I am in, therewith to be content.

—Saint Paul

Wednesday

A thankful heart is not only the greatest virtue, but the parent of all other virtues.

—Cicero

THURSDAY

When I first open my eyes upon the morning meadows and look out
upon the beautiful world, I thank God I am alive.

—Ralph Waldo Emerson

FRIDAY

Be content with what you have; rejoice in the way things are.
When you realize there is nothing lacking, the whole world belongs to you.

—Lao-Tzu

SATURDAY

The unthankful heart discovers no mercies; but the thankful heart will find, in every hour, some heavenly blessings.

—Henry Ward Beecher

Week 13

Creating Happiness

I was in high school when I first came across a quote by Abraham Lincoln suggesting that I was the person who was most responsible for my own happiness. Initially, that thought surprised me. I had believed that happiness was dependent on whether good things were happening to me. Happiness seemed to come—and go—for no apparent reason.

The idea that I could decide to be happy was incredibly empowering. I found that just declaring to myself that I wanted to be happy put me in the frame of mind to see life in a positive light.

I had stumbled upon a simple and yet powerful truth. Basically, it's not so much what happens to us in life, but how we see it that determines our happiness—or lack of it. All of us have known people who are healthy, prosperous, attractive—and miserably unhappy. In contrast are those who radiate happiness, even though they are facing enormous challenges.

Clearly, it's not how much money you make; how intelligent, attractive, or creative you are; what kind of job you have; or the status of your love life that determine your happiness. External conditions constantly change—and basing your happiness on those conditions is akin to building a foundation on quicksand.

Of course, external circumstances can contribute to feelings of happiness, but those feelings are generally short-lived unless they are rooted in gratitude and the conscious decision to see life in a positive light.

I am always inspired and uplifted by those who choose to be happy, no matter what their circumstances. What they seem to have in common is an appreciation of the tiny pleasures and gifts of life, a willingness to extend themselves to others, and a desire to look for the best in every situation. This doesn't mean you will never be unhappy, or that it's inappropriate to be sad, depressed, frustrated, or angry. But I've found it helpful for my emotional, physical, and spiritual well-being to be aware that I have a choice about how I am feeling.

This week, reflect on some of your happiest memories in life, and notice moments of happiness that occur during the week. Be aware of the interplay of your thoughts and feelings, and observe how your attitude plays a role in how happy—or unhappy—you feel.

SUNDAY

Most folks are about as happy as they make up their minds to be.

—Abraham Lincoln

MONDAY

Happiness does not depend on outward things, but on the way we see them.

—Leo Tolstoy

Tuesday

Seek not happiness too greedily, and be not fearful of unhappiness.

—Lao-Tzu

Wednesday

A happy life is one which is in accordance with its own nature.

—Seneca

THURSDAY

Happiness is a butterfly which, when pursued, is always beyond our grasp, but, if you will sit down quietly, may alight upon you.

—NATHANIEL HAWTHORNE

FRIDAY

It is not easy to find happiness in ourselves, and it is not possible to find it elsewhere.

—AGNES REPPLIER

Saturday

Happiness is not a goal, it is a by-product.

--Eleanor Roosevelt

Week 14

Rekindling Enthusiasm

Do you look forward to getting up in the morning? Do you feel a sense of happy anticipation and eagerness for what the day will bring? If you do, then you already know the joy of living with zest.

Enthusiasm is a wonderful gift of the spirit. It's contagious—taking a vital interest in life inspires those around you, and generates even greater feelings of optimism and energy. When you approach life enthusiastically, you are fully engaged and expecting the best, and the best is what you are likely to get.

Even if things don't turn out exactly as you had planned, maintaining a sense of enthusiasm enables you to experiment, explore, and try again.

In contrast, living without enthusiasm results in mechanically going through the motions of life without feeling any real pleasure or interest in what you are doing. A life without the enlivening spark of enthusiasm can become dull, mediocre, and even depressing.

This week, take time to reflect on how enthusiastic you feel about your life. What piques your interest, your passion, your sense of happiness to be alive? If you don't feel enthusiastic about much in your life, don't despair, because with attention and desire, you can rekindle your inner vitality.

To recapture enthusiasm and a sense of possibility for all that life has to offer, you must be willing to explore and to take risks. Enthusiasm naturally arises when you discover and follow your heart's desires.

Take a moment to fantasize about twenty things you would like to try. How about kayaking, bellydancing, acting, or tai chi? Perhaps nature studies, jewelry making, photography, or writing poetry spark your interest. The possibilities are infinite, and much of the delight lies in the exploration. To rekindle your enthusiasm, you must be willing to try new things and to discard those that hold little interest for you. Cultivate the habit of searching out new experiences and interests, and when you sense the spark of enthusiasm, fan it into an enduring flame.

Sunday

None are so old as those who have outlived enthusiasm.

—Henry David Thoreau

Monday

Enthusiasm is the most important thing in life.

—Tennessee Williams

Tuesday

What hunger is in relation to food, zest is in relation to life.

—Bertrand Russell

Wednesday

The world belongs to the energetic.

—Ralph Waldo Emerson

THURSDAY

You will do foolish things, but do them with enthusiasm.

—COLETTE

FRIDAY

Success is going from failure to failure without loss of enthusiasm.

—SIR WINSTON CHURCHILL

Saturday

No one keeps up his enthusiasm automatically. Enthusiasm must be nourished with new actions, new aspirations, new efforts, new vision.

—Papyrus

Week 15

Recapturing a Sense of Wonder

One of my earliest childhood memories is of standing in the sunlight in my backyard watching a wooly green-and-yellow caterpillar crawling across a leaf. I don't think I had ever seen a caterpillar before, and I was astonished and delighted at the beauty of the small creature. I couldn't have been more than two years old, and every detail of that moment is imprinted in my memory: the warm sun shining on my back, the soft grass beneath my feet, the slow movement of the caterpillar's fuzzy body, and my feeling of joy.

Children so easily connect with the wonder of life. Everything is new, and they fully embrace the delights of each moment. Each day presents infinite possibilities for exploration.

Somehow, as we grow up, we become disconnected from the sense of wonder. We begin to take things for granted. We narrow our field of vision, put our noses to the grindstone, and don't take the time to observe the magnificence of a caterpillar.

It's true that after decades of living, we've seen and done a lot, and it's easy to become jaded about caterpillars when you've seen hundreds of them. But I've noticed that when I take the time to see—as though seeing for the first time—my daily life takes on a richness and a depth that fills my heart with joy and gratitude.

The most creative people seem to have held on to—or rediscovered—their childlike sense of wonder and delight in life. Wonder opens the door to appreciation and enjoyment, and allows the creative impulses from your authentic self to bubble to the surface. The gifts of wonder are immediate: Life is transformed from a monochromatic black-and-white still life into a rich explosion of color and sensation.

This week, reflect on how often you feel a sense of wonder. How often do you take the time to really see and fully experience the magnificence that surrounds you? What early childhood memories can you recall that inspired a sense of wonder and delight in you? How might you cultivate awareness now of the wonders of daily life?

SUNDAY

There are two ways to live your life. One is as though nothing is a miracle. The other is as though everything is a miracle.

—ALBERT EINSTEIN

MONDAY

The invariable mark of wisdom is to see the miraculous in the common.

—RALPH WALDO EMERSON

TUESDAY

Today is the first day of the rest of your life.

—Abbie Hoffman

WEDNESDAY

All of us tend to put off living. We are all dreaming of some magical rose garden over the horizon instead of enjoying the roses that are blooming outside our windows today.

—Dale Carnegie

Thursday

Life is not lost by dying; life is lost minute by minute, day by day, in all the thousand small, uncaring ways.

--Stephen Saint Vincent Benét

Friday

He who can no longer pause to wonder and stand rapt in awe, is as good as dead.

--Albert Einstein

Saturday

The true mystery of the world is the visible, not the invisible.

–Oscar Wilde

Week 16

Taking Risks

We often think of risk-taking in terms of physical risks—activities like rock climbing, bungee jumping, or skydiving. But it's the emotional and creative risks we take in life that stretch our capacities and help us to become all that we are meant to be.

Living a safe life means staying within the boundaries of what we already know we can do. It's a comfortable place to be. Nothing is challenging, and it's possible to drift through life on autopilot. It's also a boring, spirit-numbing way to live.

The only way we grow is to push beyond the boundaries of what we currently regard as safe. Of course, there are times to retreat into the safety of what you know. It's wonderful to take refuge in comfort, to have a safe haven in which to rest, integrate new experiences, and renew your energy. It would be exhausting to always be living on the edge—it's a quick road to emotional and physical burnout; but to not take any risks at all means that you are passing by opportunities for change and growth.

Taking a risk can be as simple as learning a new skill, making a new friend, or trying an activity that you've never tried before. Every time you try something new, you expand your repertoire of experience and your life becomes richer and fuller. You may discover a new passion, or you might find that you're not interested in repeating the experience. What's important is that you step outside of your comfort zone to try something new.

This week, think about how you feel about taking risks. What risks have you taken, and what were the effects on your life? What kind of risks might you take now that could enrich and expand your life? What would you be willing to try? How might you benefit from taking risks?

Sunday

All serious daring starts from within.

—Eudora Welty

Monday

*Do not be too timid and squeamish. All life is an experiment.
The more experiments you make, the better.*

—Ralph Waldo Emerson

Tuesday

We must be willing to get rid of the life we've planned, so as to have the life that is waiting for us.

—Joseph Campbell

Wednesday

Make voyages. Attempt them. There's nothing else.

—Tennessee Williams

THURSDAY

Only those who risk going too far can possibly find out how far one can go.

—T. S. Eliot

FRIDAY

For of all sad words of tongue or pen the saddest are these:
It might have been.

—John Greenleaf Whittier

Saturday

It takes courage to lead a life. Any life.

--Erica Jong

Week 17

Nourishing Your Dreams

When was the last time you allowed yourself to dream? Not the dreams that come with sleep, although such dreams can provide a fascinating window into the unconscious mind. I'm referring to dreaming while you are awake, the process of allowing your authentic self to speak to you through the delicious medley of colors, images, thoughts, and feelings that arise when you allow your mind to relax and wander.

You naturally dreamed in this way as a child: dreams of adventure, of romance, of accomplishment, of fantasy and magic. Do you allow yourself the time and space to dream now?

As adults, many of us lose touch with our dreams. We regard dreaming as wasted time, time better spent accomplishing something useful. Yet, dreaming is an essential step for reconnecting with your authentic self. It's all too easy to get caught up in the daily round of life activities and to lose touch with our dreams.

Dreams—a marriage of your imagination and intuition—provide the creative raw material for fashioning your life. They offer an opportunity to try on different ways of thinking, of being, of living. Think of dreams as puttering time for your psyche, just as you might putter in your garden, in a bookstore, or at home on a Sunday afternoon. All sorts of possibilities arise in the form of dreams, seeds of ideas that you can nurture into reality if you so choose.

This week, give yourself the gift of an hour just for dreaming. Prepare an inviting space—turn off the phone, get cozy on the sofa or floor with pillows, play your favorite relaxing music, light a candle; or perhaps soak in a fragrant, warm bath.

You might even rediscover the pleasure of lying on your back in the grass, watching the clouds drift by. What's important is that you make yourself comfortable, and that you have no agenda. Nowhere to go, nothing to do except dream.

Journaling can be a valuable companion for your dream journeys— you can use your journal to record your dream images, to capture the essence of your thoughts and feelings, and to chart the path revealed by your dreams.

Sunday

Nothing happens unless first a dream.

—Carl Sandburg

Monday

Dream lofty dreams, and as you dream, so shall you become.
Your vision is the promise of what you shall at last unveil.

—John Ruskin

Tuesday

Dreams come true; without that possibility, nature would not incite us to have them.

—John Updike

Wednesday

You can't depend on your eyes when your imagination is out of focus.

—Mark Twain

Thursday

If you have built castles in the air, your work need not be lost; that is where they should be. Now put the foundations under them.

—Henry David Thoreau

Friday

Imagination has always had powers of resurrection that no science can match.

—Ingrid Bengis

Saturday

> Hold fast to dreams, for if dreams die,
> life is a broken-winged bird that cannot fly.
>
> —Langston Hughes

Accessing the Power of Action

Dreaming is essential for connecting with your soul's desires; for uncovering your true self and discovering the uniqueness of your being. But there's a step beyond dreaming that brings your images and intuition into reality; a step that helps you to manifest the life you were meant to live. The essential step that brings your dreams to life is *action*.

Dreaming without action often leads to frustration, irritability, and depression because when intuition and inspiration have no outlet for expression, they stay bottled up inside of you. Without the satisfaction of truly living your dreams, your authentic self loses hope, and your life energy ebbs.

But not just any action will do. It's somewhat of a paradox, because most of us are too busy, caught up in a daily round of activities that leave little time for self-reflection and self-nurturing. This is the place for warrior energy, for calling upon your clarity and strength to eliminate the activities that do not serve your authentic self. The action you take must breathe life into your dreams and desires.

What do you truly want to do with your life? What are the longings of your unique and wonderful being? What actions do you need to take to manifest your soul's desires?

If your desires seem too large, and the reality of manifesting your goals seems overwhelming, try breaking down your dreams into smaller manageable steps. Take one of those small steps each day of this week. Notice the renewed energy that taking action gives you. It is your authentic self thanking you for the gift of self-expression.

Sunday

The soul is made for action, and cannot rest till it be employed.

—Thomas Traherne

Monday

What you can do, or dream you can do, begin it; boldness has genius, power and magic in it.

—Johann Wolfgang von Goethe

Tuesday

An ounce of action is worth a ton of theory.

—Friedrich Engels

Wednesday

In our era, the road to holiness necessarily passes through the world of action.

—Dag Hammarskjöld

THURSDAY

*Action might not always bring happiness,
but there is no happiness without action.*

—William James

FRIDAY

Never confuse movement with action.

—Ernest Hemingway

Saturday

Go confidently in the direction of your dreams! Live the life you've imagined.

—Henry David Thoreau

Finding Support for Your Dreams

As you uncover the deepest desires of your authentic self, you might be wondering how to bring those dreams into reality. Inspiration and enthusiasm are important, but they can only carry you so far. You might feel wary if you set out with high hopes at some point in your life, but gave up those hopes when the going got difficult.

It's all too easy to attribute giving up to lack of focus or just plain laziness, but that's not true. We become discouraged and give up our dreams because no one has let us in on the secret of what it takes to be successful.

It's not hard work or discipline or luck that gets you what you want in life. Those factors do play a role, but they're minor compared to believing in yourself, taking manageable steps toward your goal, and building a support system.

You begin to manifest the desires of your authentic self at the moment you identify a heartfelt wish and take a step in the direction of your dream. At the same time, it's essential to ask for help. All too often, we set out alone to reach our goals, and believe that we have to tough it out by ourselves.

You may not have grown up in an environment that supported and nurtured you in expressing your authentic self. You may have been discouraged from really "going for it" and your dreams and desires may even have been shot down. It's not that your family wanted to deny you happiness, but if your family members didn't know how to manifest their own dreams, they certainly couldn't help you bring yours into reality. It's important to recognize, however, that it's never too late to provide a nurturing environment for yourself.

Take time this week to imagine what it would be like to have an abundance of support and encouragement as you work toward your life's desires. What would most help you to attain your goals? From whom might you seek knowledge and advice? Who can help reinforce your motivation? Who can you talk to when the going gets tough and you need a sympathetic and encouraging pep talk?

Sunday

The person who tries to live alone will not succeed as a human being. His heart withers if it does not answer another heart. His mind shrinks away if he hears only the echoes of his own thoughts and finds no other inspiration.

—Pearl S. Buck

Monday

Just as the wave cannot exist for itself, but must always participate in the swell of the ocean, so we can never experience life by ourselves, but must always share the experience of life that takes place all around us.

—Albert Schweitzer

TUESDAY

The applause of a single human being is of great consequence.

—SAMUEL JOHNSON

WEDNESDAY

Oh, the miraculous energy that flows between two people who care enough to get beyond surfaces and games, who are willing to take the risks of being totally open, of listening, of responding with the whole heart. How much we can do for each other.

—ALEX NOBLE

Thursday

Invent your world. Surround yourself with people, color, sounds, and work that nourish you.

—Sark

Friday

There is hunger for ordinary bread, and there is hunger for love, for kindness, for thoughtfulness, and this is the great poverty that makes people suffer so much.

—Mother Teresa

SATURDAY

Kindness in words creates confidence. Kindness in giving creates love.

—Lao-Tzu

Week 20

Recognizing Opportunity

Opportunities come to all of us in different ways, according to our talents, our interests, our experience, and, most of all, according to our openness to receiving them. Opportunities tend to be quiet gifts—if we don't pay close attention, we can easily overlook them.

The best way to recognize an opportunity is to cultivate a hopeful and positive attitude. Possibilities suddenly take form when you look at life from an optimistic point of view.

I know that when I become discouraged, I can't see the gifts that life is offering to me. Instead of looking outward, my vision is turned inward, my arms folded across my chest instead of openly reaching out to embrace life.

A negative outlook is based in fear—fear that the future will not bring what we long for. Fear binds our energy, and closes us down to being able to see the opportunities that surround us.

It's important to realize that opportunity comes in many different guises. It may be someone actually handing you what you desire—such as money, a job, or material possessions. More often, however, an opportunity is simply a clearing in the path for you to take a step toward realizing your authentic self.

Each day I ask for guidance, for the willingness to be open to what the day might bring. If I had held to my rigid expectations of how I thought opportunities should appear, I would have missed out on some of the most fulfilling experiences of my life.

Here are some simple truths I have learned: Do your best. Follow your heart's desires. Be open to the wonder of this moment. Ask for what you want—ask the universe, your family, your friends, yourself. Then be open to the creative ways that opportunities appear.

This week, reflect on opportunities you have received. How have those opportunities guided your life? How might you be open to more opportunities in the future?

Sunday

To improve the golden moment of opportunity,
and catch the good that is within our reach, is the great art of life.

—Samuel Johnson

Monday

When one door closes, another opens. But we often look so long and so regretfully
upon the closed door that we do not see the one which has opened for us.

—Helen Keller

Tuesday

Opportunity is missed by most people because it is dressed in overalls, and looks like work.

—Thomas Edison

Wednesday

Many things are lost for want of asking.

—English proverb

THURSDAY

*Let your hook always be cast.
In the stream where you least expect it, there will be fish.*

—Ovid

FRIDAY

The world is all gates, all opportunities, strings of tension waiting to be struck.

—Ralph Waldo Emerson

SATURDAY

Opportunities are often the things you haven't noticed the first time around.

—Catherine Deneuve

Week 21

Defining Success

We commonly gauge success in our society by the yardsticks of fame and fortune. Achieving either, or both, however, certainly doesn't guarantee a happy life—so they hardly seem good measures of success.

I like to think of success in broader terms—a life well lived and an authentic self fully expressed. When you regard success in these terms, it's well within the reach of everyone. Before you can feel successful, though, it generally takes some digging to uncover the true meaning of success for you.

It's important to identify the messages you've internalized from family, friends, and society about what constitutes success, and to reflect on your personal definition of success.

Having goals in life is important. Goals serve as guideposts and can help us to realize our heart's desires. While we commonly equate success with attaining a goal, however, it's the journey—not the goal—that is most important.

Think about how much time you spend working toward a goal, as opposed to the moment when you actually reach it. Clearly, the greatest investment of time and energy lies in the journey.

When your feelings of success are not tied solely to your achievement of a goal, you are much more likely to feel satisfied with your life. In her beautiful book *Simple Abundance*, Sarah Ban Breathnach writes, "Authentic success is having time enough to pursue personal pursuits that bring you pleasure, time enough to make the loving gestures for your family you long to do, time enough to care for your home, tend your garden, nurture your soul. Authentic success is knowing that if today were your last day on earth, you could leave without regret."

When you measure your success in the small, daily pleasures that you encounter along the way and in terms of how closely you are following the urgings of your authentic self, you will truly be living a successful life.

In what ways have you felt successful in your life? What messages have you internalized about success, and are they in alignment with the desires of your authentic self? This week, reflect on what success means to you.

Sunday

It is good to have an end to journey toward;
but it is the journey that matters, in the end.

—Ursula K. LeGuin

Monday

Success follows doing what you want to do.
There is no other way to be successful.

—Malcolm Forbes

Tuesday

The people who get on in this world are the people who get up and look for the circumstances they want, and if they can't find them, make them.

—George Bernard Shaw

Wednesday

The reward of a thing well done is to have done it.

—Ralph Waldo Emerson

THURSDAY

Authentic success is reaching the point where being is as important as doing.

—Sarah Ban Breathnach

FRIDAY

Perseverance is a great element of success. If you only knock long enough and loud enough at the gate, you are sure to wake up somebody.

—Henry Wadsworth Longfellow

SATURDAY

...To know that even one life has breathed easier because you lived. This is to have succeeded.

—Ralph Waldo Emerson

Week 22

Keeping the Faith

One of my mother's favorite sayings is, "Things always turn out for the best." Simple words, and yet I find a homey comfort and peace in reciting them during times of uncertainty or worry.

Basically, I'm calling upon my faith in myself, and choosing to see life in a positive light. When I remember to do this, I feel my body and mind relax and I am more fully available to what's taking place in the present moment.

Most people associate faith with religion, but it's not only your spiritual beliefs that benefit from faith. Cultivating faith in ourselves, others, and life brings peace of mind and prevents needless worry and anxiety from draining precious life energy. Don't, however, mistake faith for wishful thinking or a passive acceptance of whatever life dishes out.

I believe in active faith. I call on my faith to imagine my life as I want it to be, a life that is in alignment with my authentic self. I've found that nourishing faith in myself and in others tends to bring out the best. Most often, it seems that I get what I expect to get in life—and if I'm surprised, it's almost always in a positive direction.

When I have faith that the best will arise from any situation, that's what I'm likely to get. Even if my expectations are not realized in quite the way I had imagined, I lose nothing by having faith.

To lack faith is to live in negativity and fear. People who operate from doubt are always expecting the worst from every situation. While they certainly don't run the risk of being disappointed, the majority of the time their worst fears never come true. When we act from faith, we're not wasting energy in negative imaginings. Instead, we're putting all of our attention toward a positive outcome.

This week, reflect on your relationship with faith. Do you generally believe that life works out for the best, and do you have faith in yourself and others? What messages about faith and trust did your family and religious upbringing pass on to you? How might you strengthen your faith?

Sunday

Faith is a knowledge within the heart, beyond the reach of proof.

—Kahlil Gibran

Monday

Every tomorrow has two handles.
We can take hold of it with the handle of anxiety or the handle of faith.

—Henry Ward Beecher

Tuesday

It's faith in something and enthusiasm for something that makes life worth living.
—Oliver Wendell Holmes, Jr.

Wednesday

All I have seen teaches me to trust the Creator for all I have not seen.
—Ralph Waldo Emerson

Thursday

Take the first step in faith.
You don't have to see the whole staircase, just take the first step.

—Martin Luther King, Jr.

Friday

On life's journey faith is nourishment.

—Buddha

Saturday

Faith in oneself is the best and safest course.

—Michaelangelo

Week 23

Flowing with Change

Change is a powerful force in nature and in life. Without change, there is no movement or growth. Without change, there would be no variation in seasons, no rainy days or sunny days, no cycle of flowers blooming or fruits ripening.

Because there is change, we have the chance to learn from our mistakes and the opportunity to expand our knowledge and talents. Perhaps life would be safer without change, but it would also be stagnant and boring. Yet, we often resist change, fearing the unknown—or at the very least, resenting its rude intrusion.

At the opposite extreme are people who relish change. They love the turbulent energy that continual movement brings. Change becomes almost an addiction, and the amount of time and energy they spend engaged in changing jobs, homes, and relationships leaves little time for anything else in life.

In nature, the trees that best handle the challenges of change are those that are the most flexible, those that can bend and dance in a turbulent wind. They are also the trees with the deepest roots. Trees with shallow root systems, or those that are brittle and inflexible, are the most susceptible to harm from sudden windstorms.

We all encounter unexpected windstorms of change in the form of financial, relationship, work, or personal difficulties that threaten to wreak havoc with our lives. These changes may be painful challenges, but the more flexible we are and the deeper our roots of connection to our personal sources of strength and stability, the more easily we can navigate change.

This week, take time to reflect on the major changes you have experienced in your life. Were they self-generated changes? What is your style of dealing with change? Is there anything you would like to transform about the way you approach change? Take time, too, to reflect on the gifts that life changes have brought to you.

Sunday

Only in growth, reform, and change, paradoxically enough,
is true security to be found.

—Anne Morrow Lindbergh

Monday

A single day is enough to make us a little larger,
or another time, a little smaller.

—Paul Klee

Tuesday

*All things change, nothing is extinguished.
There is nothing in the whole world which is permanent.*

—Ovid

Wednesday

The changes in our life must come from the impossibility to live otherwise than according to the demands of our conscience.

—Leo Tolstoy

Thursday

You could not step twice into the same river;
for other waters are ever flowing on to you.

—Heraclitus

Friday

Every moment of one's existence one is growing into more or retreating into less.
One is always living a little more or dying a little bit.

—Norman Mailer

Saturday

Change alone is unchanging.

—Heraclitus

Week 24

Taking One Day at a Time

I felt completely overwhelmed. In the midst of a demanding home renovation project, I had also taken on a challenging writing assignment with a very short deadline. The renovation work required almost constant supervision, as well as my labor—and, of course, that wasn't all! The daily tasks of life also needed my attention—housework, cooking, running errands, paying bills.

Keeping up with all the commitments I'd made felt like an insurmountable task. When I thought of the enormity of it all, I wanted to crawl into bed and pull the covers over my head. My focus was on everything that lay ahead. Truthfully, I didn't feel up to the challenge. It seemed impossible to me that I would meet my deadline, much less that I'd ever complete the home renovations.

Then, suddenly, I remembered that I didn't have to do it all at once. I felt an enormous weight lift from my shoulders. My breathing relaxed. My mind slowed down.

I should know this by now, but sometimes I forget: Living in the future instead of taking life one day at a time is a guaranteed trip into a state of overwhelm for me. In fact, most things seem insurmountable if I forget to take them one step at a time.

Here's an analogy that a friend related to me that underscores the wisdom of taking life one day at a time: Visualize a buffet table loaded with every meal that you are going to eat for the rest of your life. Now, imagine that you have to eat all of that food today. Clearly, it's an impossible task. But meal by meal, you will eat all of that food over the course of a lifetime without any discomfort at all.

The same is true with virtually everything—taking life day by day (which is how it arrives anyway) makes it possible to reach your goals. It takes a certain amount of perseverance, but living life one day at a time makes anything doable.

This week, reflect on how you generally approach projects and goals. If you find that you get overwhelmed, anxious, or discouraged, consider how you might break down your goals into manageable steps. How can you live one day at a time?

Sunday

A journey of a thousand miles must begin with a single step.

—Chinese Proverb

Monday

Little by little does the trick.

—Aesop

Tuesday

Nothing is particularly hard if you divide it into small jobs.

—Henry Ford

Wednesday

We cannot do everything at once, but we can do something at once.

—Calvin Coolidge

Thursday

In the realm of ideas everything depends on enthusiasm; in the real world, all rests on perseverance.

—Johann Wolfgang von Goethe

Friday

When you have a great and difficult task, something perhaps almost impossible, if you only work a little at a time, every day a little, suddenly the work will finish itself.

—Isak Dinesen

Saturday

Let me tell you the secret that has led me to my goal: my strength lies solely in my tenacity.

—Louis Pasteur

Week 25

Cultivating Simplicity

Do you ever find yourself longing for a simpler way of life? A life less complex, less hurried, less demanding on your body, mind, and spirit?

The desire for simplicity is an ancient one, and a common theme of spiritual teachers, philosophers, and poets—and for good reason. Self-awareness and peace of mind can only flourish when there is the spaciousness and clarity provided by simplicity. Too many things—whether material belongings, activities, or commitments—clutter up a life.

Our days become an endless round of scrambling to keep up. With work duties, family responsibilities, household tasks, and social and community obligations, it's no wonder that many people feel there's little time for physical relaxation, much less time to nurture their mental and spiritual well-being. Yet, we need the spaciousness of unstructured time to nourish our souls and to discover what is truly most important to us in life.

Simplicity is the key to creating this spaciousness. An uncluttered environment, both internal and external, allows for serenity.

This week, take time to reflect on simplicity. What would your life be like if you had fewer obligations? What would you do with your newfound free time? What dreams and desires are you postponing because of lack of time?

You might want to make a list of all your current obligations. Look carefully at each item on your list, and evaluate which are truly necessary, and which activities and commitments enrich your life.

Consider ways in which you can simplify your life. Would you be more comfortable if you had fewer belongings cluttering up your environment? What can you let go of? What can you delegate to someone else? How can you create more spaciousness in your life?

Sunday

I believe that a simple and unassuming manner of life is best for everyone, best both for the body and the mind.

—Albert Einstein

Monday

Simplicity, simplicity, simplicity! I say let your affairs be as two or three, and not a hundred or a thousand.... Simplify, simplify.

—Henry David Thoreau

Tuesday

I am beginning to learn that it is the sweet,
simple things of life which are the real ones after all.

—Laura Ingalls Wilder

Wednesday

Eat when you're hungry. Drink when you're thirsty. Sleep when you're tired.

—Buddhist proverb

Thursday

Voluntary simplicity means going fewer places in one day rather than more, seeing less so I can see more, doing less so I can do more, acquiring less so I can have more.

—Jon Kabat-Zinn

Friday

Life is not complex. We are complex. Life is simple, and the simple thing is the right way.

—Oscar Wilde

Saturday

I have a simple philosophy. Fill what's empty. Empty what's full. Scratch where it itches.

—Alice Roosevelt Longworth

Week 26

The Joy of Learning

I spent almost twenty years of my life in school, from kindergarten through graduate school. Except for my two years of graduate school, I invested just enough effort to keep up my grades. I'm not proud of this. But I wasn't interested in most of what I had to study—and, consequently, I found little joy in learning.

Fortunately my learning didn't stop when I left school. In fact, my education began in earnest once I left traditional schools behind. Given the freedom to explore, I began to study herbal medicine, natural healing, organic gardening, yoga, and meditation.

None of these subjects were offered as classes in the schools I attended. The topics were considered, at best, off-beat, and they certainly were not marketable interests in the mid-1970s. Yet, by following the passions of my authentic self, I've successfully created a career as a writer and teacher in the field of natural health.

Learning comes quickly and easily when you follow the questing of your authentic self. Because you are studying what you truly want to know, learning becomes virtually effortless—almost like a deep remembering of ancient knowledge that you already possess. This type of learning feeds the hunger for the knowledge and skills that your authentic self needs for full expression.

One of the great benefits of lifelong learning is that it keeps life continually interesting. We all have innate curiosity about ourselves, others, and our environment. The desire for knowledge never fades, but it can certainly be submerged if we are discouraged by years of institutionalized schooling. You are taught in most educational institutions to ignore the desires of your authentic self in favor of what is deemed necessary for you to learn.

This week, use the pages of this journal to discover what your authentic self is hungering to learn. Imagine that you have the time and opportunity to freely explore what interests you. What are some things that you truly want to learn? What knowledge and skills would enrich and expand your life?

Sunday

A mind that is stretched to a new idea never returns to its original dimension.

—Oliver Wendell Holmes, Jr.

Monday

Learning is movement from moment to moment.

—J. Krishnamurti

Tuesday

Everyone and everything around you is your teacher.

—Ken Keyes, Jr.

Wednesday

You are never too old to set another goal or to dream a new dream.

—Les Brown

Thursday

As long as you live, keep learning how to live.

—Seneca

Friday

Anyone who stops learning is old, whether at 20 or 80. Anyone who keeps learning stays young. The greatest thing in life is to keep your mind young.

—Henry Ford

SATURDAY

To be surprised, to wonder, is to begin to understand.

—José Ortega y Gasset

Week 27

Finding Your Life's Work

We live in a society that greatly values work. We grow up expecting to work, and are taught that through working hard, we may be able to achieve financial and material success. But rarely are we taught that work provides the opportunity to fulfill our life's dreams and our heart's desires.

For most of us, the majority of our waking hours are spent at work. If you don't love what you are doing, it's time to reevaluate how you are spending your precious life energy, time, and skills.

Many people work just to pay the bills, and make a clear distinction between work and play. If that's the way you regard your work, then the activities that provide enjoyment or allow you to be creative may lie outside the realm of worklife—assuming you have time and energy left over to pursue those activities.

The work you do can meet not only your material needs, but your needs for creativity and enjoyment as well. In her inspirational book *Living in the Light*, Shakti Gawain writes, "Work is no longer something you have to do in order to sustain life. Instead, the delight that comes from expressing yourself becomes the greatest reward."

What you choose as your life's work offers you the opportunity to fully express your talents and interests, and gives you the chance to make a unique contribution to the world.

If you are now in a job that you find boring or unpleasant, it's time to think seriously about how you can make a shift into something that will fulfill your authentic self. The first step is knowing what you love to do. Then take the steps necessary to bring your dream into reality.

If you're not really certain of what you love, don't despair. The seeds of what you love are within you, and are simply waiting for your encouragement and attention before they begin to grow.

There are many ways to transition into work that you find more satisfying. In her helpful book, *It's Only Too Late if You Don't Start Now*, Barbara Sher offers a number of suggestions for creating the work you want. Scale down your current job, she suggests, or take a sabbatical. You might moonlight doing something you love or find a way to tailor your present job so that it meets your interests. The important point is to realize that you always have alternatives.

This week, think about your work and how you feel about it. If you could do anything at all during your working hours, what would you do? What special gifts and talents do you have? Can you imagine creating work that would use your unique talents? What would it take for you to make your ideal job a reality?

Sunday

Work and play can be the same. When you are following your energy and doing what you want to do all the time, the distinction between work and play dissolves.

—Shakti Gawain

Monday

There is a vitality, a life force, an energy, a quickening, that is translated through you into action, and because there is only one of you in all time, this expression is unique. And if you block it, it will never exist through any other medium and will be lost.

—Martha Graham

Tuesday

Love and work are the cornerstones of our humanness.

—Sigmund Freud

Wednesday

Let the beauty we love be what we do.

—Rumi

THURSDAY

Are you bored with life? Then throw yourself into some work you believe in with all your heart and you will find happiness that you had thought could never be yours.

—Dale Carnegie

FRIDAY

Remember that you are needed. There is at least one important work to be done that will not be done unless you do it.

—Charles L. Allen

Saturday

We are shaped and fashioned by what we love.

—Johann Wolfgang von Goethe

Week 28

Remembering How to Play

For many of us, playtime ends when we put away our childhood toys. Although it's natural to lose interest in the type of play we engaged in as children, however, we never lose our *need* for play.

Play provides relaxation, fun, and enjoyment. Equally important, play gives us the meandering time necessary for creative impulses to surface. Merging the child's natural inclination to play with the freedom that comes with adulthood affords unlimited potential for creativity and self-expression.

Some of the most brilliant, creative people I know are so adept at playing that they regard their work as play. If you are following the urgings of your authentic self, you'll become familiar with that feeling. What is play, after all, but immersing yourself in what you love to do?

Just as when we were children, play prepares us for life. Not only is it fun, but it gives us the opportunity to experiment with new activities and new ways of expressing ourselves.

As adults we too often limit ourselves to passive forms of entertainment, such as watching movies or television; reading magazines; or attending sports events, theatre, or music performances. While these can be fun and enriching ways to spend time, play is most creative when we are actively involved instead of sitting on the sidelines.

If you are always a spectator, you lose out on the possibility of learning something new. As a participant, you engage your creativity and expand your repertoire of skills and experiences.

This week, remember your favorite ways of playing as a child. What are your favorite ways of playing *now*? To prompt your creative, playful self, make a list of at least a dozen things you think would be fun to try.

Sunday

We don't stop playing because we grow old; we grow old because we stop playing.

—George Bernard Shaw

Monday

Each day, and the living of it, has to be a conscious creation in which discipline and order are relieved with some play and pure foolishness.

—May Sarton

Tuesday

We should consider every day lost on which we have not danced at least once.

—Friedrich Nietzsche

Wednesday

Play is the exultation of the possible.

—Martin Buber

THURSDAY

Live a balanced life—learn some and think some and draw and paint and sing and dance and play and work every day some.

—Robert Fulghum

FRIDAY

The creation of something new is not accomplished by the intellect but by the play instinct.

—Carl Jung

SATURDAY

Life must be lived as play.

—Plato

Week 29

Seeking Adventure

I have always loved to travel. For months at a time, I have sought the adventure of new places, people, and experiences. Hiking the canyons of the Southwest, swimming in the Adriatic Sea, exploring villages in Portugal and monasteries in Serbia, soaking in Turkish baths in Hungary—these are all adventures that have immeasurably enriched my life.

But while I still love the adventure of travel, I've realized that what I enjoy most about traveling is the way it awakens me to the extraordinary in daily life. Every day is an adventure when I'm traveling. The sensory delight of unfamiliar landscapes, architecture, and people; foreign languages; exotic foods, smells, colors, and sounds combine to arouse my senses so that I can be nowhere but fully present in the moment.

This is the core of the thrill of adventure. It quickens our life force and awakens us to the fullness of this moment, with all of its possibilities.

I've realized, however, that while adventure often comes through travel, it also comes from traveling inside ourselves. Inner exploration helps us discover and uncover our hidden talents, dreams, and desires.

There is no greater adventure we can embark upon than the journey to our authentic selves.

I've also realized that life, in and of itself, is an adventure. Each day, if we are open to it, offers infinite possibilities. It doesn't matter if today looks on the surface very similar to yesterday, or the day before—this day is unique, and if we are awake to it, there will be unexpected gifts.

Adventure isn't only rafting the Colorado River or trekking in Tibet—it's the spirit in which we approach daily life. Every day presents us with new opportunities and challenges, and gives us the chance to discover more about ourselves.

This week, reflect on adventures you have had in your life. What did you learn about yourself through your adventures? What adventures intrigue you now? Can you imagine approaching your daily life in a spirit of adventure?

SUNDAY

Life is either a daring adventure or nothing.

—HELEN KELLER

MONDAY

There is only one journey. Going inside yourself.

—RANIER MARIA RILKE

TUESDAY

It is only in adventure that some people succeed in knowing themselves—in finding themselves.

—André Gide

WEDNESDAY

An adventure is only an inconvenience rightly considered.

—G. K. Chesterton

Thursday

When you've got your sense of wonder back...your whole life can be full of adventure.

—Barbara Sher

Friday

The most precious gift to bring back from a journey is the ability to see the extraordinary in the everyday.

—Eric Hansen

Saturday

One does not discover new lands without consenting to lose sight of the shore for a very long time.

—Andre Gide

Week 30

Making Time for Pleasure

I love pleasure. In fact, I put pleasure at the top of my "to do" list, and I make sure that I do at least a couple of things every day that bring me enjoyment.

I didn't always make pleasure a high priority. I used to believe that the pursuit of pleasure was somewhat self-indulgent, and I thought I should be doing more important things with my life. I never did figure out what those more important things were, but I finally realized that pleasure is a gift freely given by the Universe. Why else would there be the fragrance of roses and lilacs, the beauty of sunrises and sunsets, the exquisite sensation of a loving caress?

Seeking and finding pleasure in life refills the well of the spirit and nourishes the authentic self. Now, the amount of pleasure I experience is one of my guideposts for measuring how closely I am living in harmony with my authentic self. I've come to realize that the more open I am to receiving pleasure, the more I embody joy, gratitude, and generosity of spirit.

Interestingly, it's rarely the big things in life—the promotions, material possessions, fame, or fortune—that bring lasting pleasure. More often, enjoyment comes from the simple pleasures that are easily woven into daily life. These are the pleasures that provide constant nourishment for the body and soul.

Among my simple pleasures I include long walks, planting flowers, harvesting vegetables and herbs from my garden, soaking in an aromatherapy bath, reading a good book, painting with watercolors, and having tea with a friend.

Actually, I've found that the experience of pleasure is more an attitude than an acquisition. It's a grateful acceptance of the beauty and the small gifts of life that uplift the spirit.

Pleasure takes many forms, but all spring from the authentic self. The things that bring you pleasure are unique to you. The more you nourish yourself with these delights, the more energy and zest you will have for life.

This week, you might want to make a list of at least two dozen things that bring you pleasure. When was the last time you experienced each item on your list? How might you bring more pleasure into your daily life?

Sunday

The giving and receiving of pleasure is a need and an ecstasy.

—Kahlil Gibran

Monday

Pleasure is very seldom found where it is sought; our brightest blazes of gladness are commonly kindled by unexpected sparks.

—Samuel Johnson

Tuesday

The world has to learn that the actual pleasure derived from material things is of rather low quality on the whole and less even in quantity than it looks to those who have not tried it.

—Oliver Wendell Holmes, Sr.

Wednesday

That man is richest whose pleasures are cheapest.

—Henry David Thoreau

Thursday

Happiness consists more in small conveniences or pleasures that occur every day, than in great pieces of good fortune that happen but seldom.

—Benjamin Franklin

Friday

*Why not seize the pleasure at once?
How often is happiness destroyed by preparation, foolish preparation?*

—Jane Austen

Saturday

If you always do what interests you, at least one person is pleased.

—Katharine Hepburn

Week 31

Embracing Your Sensuality

We register the world around us with our five senses Those senses, however, are much more than a simple connection to the external environment. Exploring the realm of your senses will take you unerringly to the core of your authentic self.

The dimensions of what you find most pleasurable are an expression of the uniqueness of your being. Cultivating an appreciation of your sensuality will help you to create a life that is distinctively yours, and will give you great pleasure along the way.

Few of us, I suspect, are completely comfortable with the idea of making sensual pleasures a high priority. But we were born with the gift of our five senses, and enjoying the pleasures that they offer can be a spiritual practice that awakens us to the magnificence of life.

At the very moment I'm writing these words, I am delighting in my senses—the fragrance of roses and lavender, the caress of a warm summer breeze, the melodious song of a warbler. I am struck by the beauty of the vibrant blue delphiniums that are blooming in my garden. I pause to taste the sweet juiciness of a sun-ripened peach. This is the sacredness of daily life.

We need to allow ourselves to fully open to the sensuality of our beings. Each day of this week, take time to pay attention to the details of life, as relayed to you by your senses. Be awake to the present moment. Use all the sensual powers you have—to taste, touch, see, smell, and hear.

Sunday

But what minutes! Count them by sensation, and not by calendars, and each moment is a day.

—Benjamin Disraeli

Monday

As we open to our own sensuality we experience more of the passion for life.

—Shakti Gawain

Tuesday

I'm passionately involved in life. I love its change, its color, its movements. To be able to speak, to see, to hear, to walk, to have music and paintings...it is all a miracle.

—Arthur Rubinstein

Wednesday

Life is a romantic business, but you have to make the romance.

—Oliver Wendell Holmes, Sr.

Thursday

The aim of life is to live, and to live means to be aware, joyously, drunkenly, serenely, divinely aware.

—Henry Miller

Friday

Paradise is where I am.

—Voltaire

Saturday

Freeing the body inevitably leads to freeing the heart.

—Gabrielle Roth

Week 32

The Art of Seeing

We tend to rely on our sense of sight more than any of our other senses to process information about the world around us. But how much do we really see? Most of the time, the world passes by in a blur of preconceived images.

Really *seeing* something takes time and a shift of awareness. I'm learning this lesson well while struggling to refine my drawing and painting skills. I think I know what an iris looks like. I've grown irises, and have enjoyed their beauty for years. I can recognize one in an instant. But I couldn't begin to draw an iris without having one in front of me, and even then, it's an enormously difficult task.

For the first time, I really see an iris. I see the faint sprinkling of magenta freckles on the pale lavender petals and the edging of deep, velvety purple; the fuzzy caterpillar-like yellow stamen; the papery covering of the bud. I am overwhelmed by the details, and, at the same time, totally immersed in this singular, unique iris.

I look more closely in my garden at the flowers I take for granted—the lavender and apricot roses, magenta bee balm, indigo spikes of veronica. Apples are ripening with a delicate blush of rose staining their golden skins. Strawberries like scarlet jewels peek out from beneath emerald green clusters of leaves—I pluck several, and notice that while each one is recognizable as a strawberry, none fit my preconceived image of a strawberry.

The variety of form and color in life is astonishing. We create categories in our brains because it makes life simpler. Once we have a general idea of what a strawberry looks like, we make up a generic image that we superimpose over every strawberry we come across. This keeps us from becoming bogged down in the details of examining everything that enters our visual field. Every so often, however, it's inspiring, invigorating, and nourishing to the soul to awaken to the details that surround us.

Take a piece of fruit, a flower, an object you love, the face of a loved one, and really look at it. What is it like for you to see in this way?

Sunday

When the eye wakes up to see again, it stops taking anything for granted.

—Frederick Franck

Monday

In a way nobody sees a flower really, it is so small, we haven't the time, and to see takes time.

—Georgia O'Keeffe

TUESDAY

Learn to see, and then you'll know that there is no end to the new worlds for our vision.

—Carlos Casteneda

WEDNESDAY

The greatest thing a human being ever does in this world is to see something. To see clearly is poetry, prophecy and religion, all in one.

—John Ruskin

Thursday

When your life is filled with the desire to see the holiness in everyday life, something magical happens: Ordinary life becomes extraordinary, and the very process of life begins to nourish your soul!

—Rabbi Harold Kushner

Friday

The real voyage of discovery consists not in seeking new landscapes, but in having new eyes.

—Marcel Proust

Saturday

It is looking at things for a long time that ripens you and gives you a deeper understanding.

—Vincent van Gogh

Week 33

Attuning to Sound

Sound infuses and surrounds us, much of it uninvited, some welcome, some not so welcome. I tune in to the sound of the wind gently rustling the leaves of the oak tree outside my window, a robin softly chirping to its fledgling, my partner laughing with his daughter in the next room, the faint melody of Celtic music weaving everything together.

I listen more deeply and am aware of the hum of traffic noises bouncing off the mountains from miles away, a sound that disturbs me if I pay close attention.

Sounds affect us deeply, perhaps more than we realize. Sound soothes, heals, invigorates, relaxes, inspires, and agitates. It goes deeply into the core of our beings and stirs our bodies and souls.

Sound and music have been used throughout the ages to induce a state of meditation. Drumming, chanting, and other forms of voice and instrument rhythms facilitate inner journeys for healing, renewal, and self-understanding. "Perhaps more than any sense except smell, sound bypasses our rational mind to move us at a primal level," writes creativity teacher Julia Cameron in her book *The Vein of Gold*.

At the other end of the spectrum, the absence of sound, or silence, grants us the gift of sensory spaciousness. When we can hear nothing else, we have an opportunity to hear our inner voice, speaking from the authentic self. "Silence is how we catch our breath," writes Cameron. "Silence is how we hear ourselves think, and also how we can hear the still, small voice speaking within us."

This week, notice in your daily life the various sounds and the moments of silence that permeate your days and nights. You might wish to experiment with music, playing different types and taking note of the effects. Experiment with silence, too, giving yourself at least an hour of uninterrupted quiet. Notice how you feel.

SUNDAY

There is nothing better than music as a means for the upliftment of the soul.

—HAZRAT INAYAT KHAN

___

MONDAY

Your voice takes you to your heart.

—GABRIELLE ROTH

TUESDAY

And silence, like a poultice comes to heal the blows of sound.

—Oliver Wendell Holmes, Sr.

WEDNESDAY

Music has the capacity to touch the innermost reaches of the soul and music gives flight to the imagination.

—Plato

Thursday

We need silence to be able to touch souls.

—Mother Teresa

Friday

After silence, that which comes nearest to expressing the inexpressible is music.

—Aldous Huxley

Saturday

> When we pay attention to nature's music, we find that everything on the earth contributes to its harmony.
>
> —Hazrat Inayat Khan

Week 34

The Delights of Fragrance

Your sense of smell influences your emotional well-being more powerfully than your sight, your hearing, or your sense of taste or touch. Because your sense of smell arises from the same part of your brain that houses your emotions, memories, and sensuality, smells directly affect your moods. That's why a whiff of cinnamon instantaneously calls up memories of holiday celebrations, or the scent of fresh-mown grass recalls lazy, warm summer days from childhood. This direct access to emotions offers a wonderful opportunity to use scent to positively influence your well-being on a daily basis.

Take a moment right now to notice the scents surrounding you. Are there perfumes or flowers permeating the air? Odors from cleaning or laundry products? Smells of food cooking? Is there a fresh, clean scent, or an underlying mustiness? Do you like the fragrances and odors that surround you?

This week, be aware of the scents you encounter, and make a note of those you find especially pleasing. Begin to cultivate the habit of bringing the scents that make you feel good into your daily life.

You might want to start by clearing out your home and work space, opening the windows every day to allow fresh air to blow away stale odors and mustiness. Bring fresh flowers into your home and office. Keep a vial of peppermint or basil aromatherapy essential oil by your desk and take a whiff when you need a quick pick-me-up.

Begin and end your day by burning mild incense or scented aromatherapy candles. Soak in baths with aromatherapy essential oils. Add ten drops of marjoram for a relaxing bath, try sandalwood for sensuality, or use lavender to uplift your mood. Experiment with body lotions, soaps, and shampoos scented with other essential oils.

Perfume your bed linens, closets, and dresser drawers with sachets filled with fragrant herbs. Drink a mug of hot apple cider simmered with cinnamon sticks, or a cup of spicy and fragrant ginger tea. Go to sleep at night with a small dream pillow filled with lavender flowers, rose petals, and chamomile blossoms. Notice the effects that various scents have on your moods and feelings, and journal about your observations.

Sunday

*Nothing can cure the soul but the senses,
just as nothing can cure the senses but the soul.*

—Oscar Wilde

Monday

*Smell is a potent wizard that transports us
across thousands of miles and all the years we have lived.*

—Helen Keller

Tuesday

You're only here for a short visit. Don't hurry. Don't worry. And be sure to smell the flowers along the way.

—Walter Hagen

Wednesday

If I had but two loaves of bread, I would sell one and buy hyacinths, for they would feed my soul.

—The Koran

THURSDAY

The best things are nearest: breath in your nostrils, light in your eyes, flowers at your feet.

—Robert Louis Stevenson

FRIDAY

Smells are surer than sounds and sights to make heartstrings crack.

—Rudyard Kipling

Saturday

For the sense of smell, almost more than any other, has the power to recall memories and it's a pity that we use it so little.

—Rachel Carson

Week 35

The Healing Pleasure of Touch

Touch is not only pleasurable, it is essential to our well being. Many research studies have shown that people become depressed, anxious, and are more likely to fall ill if they are deprived of touch.

For something that feels so good, it's strange that we don't indulge more in our need to touch and be touched. Many of us are touch-starved without consciously knowing it. We confuse touch with sex, and while touch is certainly integral to sexual connection, that's not the only appropriate role for touch in our lives.

I've worked in the field of healing for years, and yet it has only been in the past couple of years that I've allowed myself the healing and restorative benefits of a massage every month. My massage therapist refers to her work as a "necessary luxury," and she's right. I feel completely renewed after a massage. I consider it so important to my well-being that I now calculate it as a regular expense in my budget. Exchanging foot, neck, and shoulder massages with your partner or a friend is another wonderful way to enjoy the healing pleasure of touch.

In addition to massage and human touch, there are many other ways of appreciating the pleasures that the sense of touch provides. Some of my most enjoyable childhood memories are of floating motionless in the warm waters of the Florida Keys, completely supported by the buoyancy of the water. I also cherish sensory memories of the refreshing, cool surprise of the Adriatic Sea, and recall with pleasure what it feels like to soak in the deeply relaxing mineral waters of a California hot spring. The feel of a richly textured fabric, stroking a cat's fur, and walking barefoot on soft grass or a sandy beach all indulge the wonderful, sensory pleasure of touch.

How might you bring more of the pleasure of touch into your life? This week, schedule a massage for yourself or exchange foot and neck rubs with a friend. Hug loved ones. Walk barefoot in the grass. Wear silk or velvet. Seek out sensory experiences that engage your awareness of touch. Notice how you feel.

SUNDAY

Loving touch is a wonderful, comforting, healing form of connection.

—Andrew Weil, M.D.

MONDAY

Above all, touch teaches us that life has depth and contour;
it makes our sense of the world and ourself three-dimensional.

—Diane Ackerman

TUESDAY

It is a mistake to believe that we ever outgrow the primal need to touch and be touched.

—SAM KEEN

WEDNESDAY

The first sense to ignite, touch is often the last to burn out.

—FREDERICK SACHS

THURSDAY

Touch is the only sense we cannot live without.

— Michael Castleman

FRIDAY

Seeing, hearing and feeling are miracles, and each part and tag of me is a miracle.

—Walt Whitman

Saturday

Good hugs are therapeutic. They can restore the feeling of being cherished and protected—that primal, wordless sense of security and well-being that we innocently demanded as children, but rarely allow ourselves to experience as adults.

—Margo Anand

Nourishment for the Body and Soul

Food does much more than fill the stomach and fuel the body: It provides pleasure as well as nourishment for the senses and the soul. Dining together is one of the primary ways in which we celebrate life with family and friends.

We renew our life force and our connection to the earth with every meal. Food "is a big source of pleasure in most lives, a complex realm of satisfaction both physiological and emotional, much of which involves memories of childhood," writes naturalist and poet Diane Ackerman in her fascinating book *Natural History of the Senses*.

Food provides a direct connection to the heart and soul through memories. Think of the comforting foods of home and childhood, the exotic foods of travels, the meals shared with friends and family.

Tastes linger in memory long after the meal has been eaten and digested. I can recall in a split second the spiciness of fish stew in a Budapest cafe. I tried homemade goat cheese with an unforgettable, pungent flavor in the mountains of Serbia. Give me another moment, and I can recall smoky sardines grilled over a wood fire in Portugal, thick creamy yogurt drizzled with honey eaten at an outdoor cafe in Athens, crusty bread from a bakery in Provence.

On a trip back to Florida last year, my mom cooked flounder stuffed with crabmeat, Gulf shrimp sauteed in butter and garlic, and Oysters Rockefeller. Yes, these foods nourished my body. But they did more—satisfying my craving for the familiar foods of home.

Well-prepared food brings pleasure to all who partake of it. When you choose the freshest seasonal foods and prepare them with love, you are offering a gift to yourself and others. Eating those foods is a sacred act, a celebration of life, a ritual through which we renew ourselves each day.

As you journal this week, reflect on the role that food and your sense of taste play in your life. Recall the tastes of comforting childhood foods—favorite foods associated with celebrations—exotic tastes from travels. What foods and tastes do you crave? How might you bring more awareness and enjoyment to the act of preparing and eating food?

SUNDAY

> Any time we eat it's holy. We should have ritual and ceremony,
> not just gobbling down some food to keep alive.
>
> —M.F.K. Fisher

MONDAY

> The art of cooking, of using fire, water, and salt,
> is the art of alchemy in the kitchen.
>
> —Cecile Tovah Levin

Tuesday

All eating is communion, feeding the soul as well as the body.

—Thomas Moore

Wednesday

May I awaken to what these ingredients offer, and may I awaken, as best I can, energy, warmth, imagination, this offering of heart and hand.

—Edward Espe Brown

Thursday

It is an illusion to think of food as something that we consume simply for calories and nutrients. Food is central to the celebration of life and the soul of humanity's social life.

—Ron Pickarski

Friday

Cooking is like love. It should be entered into with abandon or not at all.

—Harriet Van Horne

Saturday

Joining with family or friends to prepare a festive meal can be as nourishing to body and mind as the food itself.

—Deborah Madison

Week 37

Appreciating Beauty

The creation and appreciation of beauty often sink to the bottom of the list in the hierarchy of what is considered important in life. Taking care of business, making a living, tending to family and home, and all of the other tasks of keeping daily life together may seem to leave little time for the pursuit of beauty. Taking time for beauty may even be regarded as frivolous if you consider other things more important.

But what if the enjoyment of beauty *is* a necessity? "The assumption that beauty is an accessory, and dispensable, shows that we don't understand the importance of giving the soul what it needs," writes psychotherapist and theologian Thomas Moore in his thought-provoking book, *Care of the Soul*. "The soul is nurtured by beauty. What food is to the body, arresting, complex, and pleasing images are to the soul."

I love creating beauty in my life and feel that beauty does, indeed, feed my soul. Not long ago, however, I fell prey to feeling vaguely uneasy about the amount of time and energy I had expended during almost two years of transforming an ugly, neglected house into my vision of a beautiful home and gardens.

When I confided to a friend (whom I also consider a spiritual teacher) that the pursuit of so much beauty felt selfish, her response was clear and immediate. "You have created a home that at this moment is nourishing my soul," she said gently. I was deeply touched that my attention to creating beauty was nurturing her soul as well as mine, and realized that beauty is a gift to all who come in contact with it.

Beauty does nourish the soul—it awakens us to the magnificence of life, and encourages the creative pursuits of the authentic self. The contemplation of what is beautiful provides a resting place for the spirit. It takes us out of the businesslike, technological world in which we live, and inspires us to celebrate the beauty of nature and the incredible creativity of the human spirit.

Developing an appreciation for beauty and discovering what resonates with your unique being is a delightful journey in life. If you don't already do so, consider treating yourself to regular excursions to feed your soul's desire for beauty. You might try exploring beautiful places in nature, art museums, art and craft galleries, gardens, and whatever else catches your fancy.

This week, open your eyes and your soul to the beauty that surrounds you. What speaks to your soul? Are there ways that you can imagine bringing more beauty into your life?

Sunday

The human soul needs actual beauty more than bread.

—D. H. Lawrence

Monday

The best and most beautiful things in the world cannot be seen or even touched—they must be felt with the heart.

—Helen Keller

Tuesday

*There is certainly no absolute standard of beauty.
That precisely is what makes its pursuit so interesting.*

—John Kenneth Galbraith

Wednesday

*A thing of beauty is a joy forever; Its loveliness increases;
it will never pass into nothingness.*

—John Keats

THURSDAY

*Things are pretty, graceful, rich, elegant, handsome,
but until they speak to the imagination, not yet beautiful.*

—Ralph Waldo Emerson

FRIDAY

Everything has beauty, but not everyone sees it.

—Confucius

SATURDAY

There is nothing that makes its way more directly to the soul than beauty.

—Joseph Addison

Week 38

Reconnecting with Nature

Nature offers infinite opportunities for renewal, and is always available to soothe, refresh, and restore our bodies, minds, and spirits. It takes only the willingness to venture outdoors and the intention to awaken your senses to the magnificence that surrounds you.

What special places in nature have you loved? Take a moment to reflect on your favorite spots. Perhaps the forest calls to you in the gentle rustling of leaves in the wind and the fragrance of pine needles and herbs. Maybe you have a favorite boulder in the middle of a clear, rushing creek that is the perfect spot on a hot summer's day. Possibly, what you love most is walking along a secluded beach, allowing the rhythmic sound of the waves to lull you into tranquility.

Collect these mental images of your favorite natural sanctuaries, and call upon them at times when you need the restorative peace of nature.

Try to spend some time every day in nature, even if only for a half hour. Seek out places that speak to your soul. Visit them often. If you live in the country or a small town, it should be easy to find places where nature thrives undisturbed. Even if you live in a big city, search out parks and other natural spots and discover your favorite places to adopt as your own.

You might even consider creating a small nature sanctuary in your own backyard. Plant flowers and herbs for their color, fragrance, and beauty. Before long, you will be seeing other creatures in this environment—bees, birds, and butterflies that are drawn to any garden, however small. Furnish your sanctuary with a birdbath, birdfeeders, and a comfortable place for you to sit and observe.

If you feel you have lost your connection to nature—if there are pleasures and sensations that you've forgotten—this is the week to make contact again. Take a walk outdoors in a beautiful natural place. Observe the magnificence of towering trees, the beauty of wildflowers in bloom, the joyous singing of birds, and the miracle of a brightly colored butterfly floating lazily by. The gifts of nature are abundant, and ever changing.

Sunday

Forget not that the earth delights to feel your bare feet and the winds long to play with your hair.

—Kahlil Gibran

Monday

I believe a leaf of grass is no less than the journey-work of the stars.

—Walt Whitman

TUESDAY

We can never have enough of nature. We need to witness our own limitations transgressed, and some life pasturing freely where we never wander.

—Henry David Thoreau

WEDNESDAY

The day, water, sun, moon, night—I do not have to purchase these things with money.

—Plautus

Thursday

To see a World in a Grain of Sand and a Heaven in a Wild Flower, hold Infinity in the palm of your hand and Eternity in an Hour.

—William Blake

Friday

All my life through, the new sights of nature made me rejoice like a child.

—Marie Curie

Saturday

Keep close to Nature's heart...and break clear away once in a while, and climb a mountain or spend a week in the woods. Wash your spirit clean.

—John Muir

Week 39

Living Abundantly

Is there anyone that at times doesn't long for more money? Don't you think, at least on occasion, that if you only had more money you would be happier, more fulfilled, freer, and more relaxed?

"The truth, is, of course, that happiness is an inside job, and beyond the subsistence level, money truly has very little to do with our happiness," writes M. J. Ryan in her book of meditations, *Attitudes of Gratitude*.

I've noticed a curious thing about my relationship with money. It seems that the more I have, the more I up the ante for what I think I need. I've observed a similar dynamic in my approach to the material possessions and luxuries that money allows me to buy. The object that I desire, once purchased, gives me a few hours or days of delight. But after that, I am soon attracted to another object I think I must own. That one, I'm sure, will make me happy and I'll not want anything again for a very long time (or so my thinking goes).

Not that there's anything wrong with having desires. We can't rid ourselves of the need for material possessions, and I don't think that we should try. But to equate happiness and fulfillment with the amount of money in our bank accounts or the number of items we buy is self-destructive.

If we don't feel what we have now is enough, no amount more is ever going to be sufficient. The well we are trying to fill with money and material possessions is a bottomless pit if we are not filling it from the inside with appreciation for what we already have.

It's important to recognize that money is simply a medium of exchange. Money can be exchanged for leisure, fun, beauty, luxury, comfort, and freedom. But there are many ways to fulfill these desires that don't involve money—or require much less money than we imagine. Abundance is a gift that we give to ourselves, and it has more to do with our attitude and approach to life than how much we have materially.

In the book *Your Money or Your Life*, authors Joe Dominguez and Vicki Robin make the point that money is a direct exchange for life energy. Reading that book has certainly changed the way I think about money—for everything I am tempted to buy, I first consider how much I am actually spending in terms of my precious life energy and time. It helps to bring my wants more into alignment with my true needs and desires.

This week, reflect on your relationship to money. Are you spending your money—actually your life energy—on what is truly most important to you? What desires are you trying to fulfill with money? What are some other ways you might meet these desires?

Sunday

One of our difficulties is that too often we confuse
spiritual yearnings with material wants.

—Sarah Ban Breathnach

Monday

Life begets life. Energy creates energy.
It is by spending oneself that one becomes rich.

—Sarah Bernhardt

Tuesday

Money is something we choose to trade our life energy for...our choices about how we use it express the meaning and purpose of our time here on earth.

—Joe Dominguez and Vicki Robin

Wednesday

Always leave enough time in your life to do something that makes you happy, satisfied, even joyous. That has more of an effect on economic well-being than any other single factor.

—Paul Hawken

Thursday

*What we really want to do is what we are really meant to do.
When we do what we are meant to do, money comes to us,
doors open for us, we feel useful, and the work we do feels like play to us.*

—Julia Cameron

Friday

*If you seek what is honorable, what is good, what is the truth of your life,
all the other things you could not imagine come as a matter of course.*

—Oprah Winfrey

Saturday

Do what you love, and the money will follow.

—Marsha Sinetar

Week 40

Engaging Your Imagination

For more than twenty years I've kept a daily journal, using writing as a tool to clear my mind, develop self-understanding, and connect with my authentic self. One of the greatest gifts of my journaling has been to keep me on track, following my inner wisdom and helping me to live the life that is in alignment with my innermost desires.

Occasionally I read back over my journals, and I'm struck by how they have been an accurate predictor of how my life has unfolded. When I was in my twenties, I envisioned and journaled about my desire to live in a beautiful, small mountain town and to make my living as a writer. I didn't know how it would happen—I had no training as a writer and had lived all of my life in Florida. Through a circuitous journey that first took me to Houston, Boston, Europe, and southern California, however, I found myself by the age of forty living in a small, beautiful mountain town in Oregon and supporting myself as a writer.

This is only one example of the imaginings I have journaled about that have become reality. This process isn't magic, but is the natural consequence of uncovering our true desires and imagining ourselves in the place of realizing our dreams. When we engage our imagination and visualize our lives as we want them to be, we open ourselves to the possibilities that are presented to us on a daily basis. A part of our consciousness also actively begins to seek out opportunities to bring our dreams into reality.

There are many intriguing and fun ways to engage the power of imagination. I've used exercises from Shakti Gawain's wonderful book, *Creative Visualization,* for years. One of my favorites is to create a treasure map, which involves making a collage of an area of your life (such as relationships, work, creativity, or health) with pictures, words, photographs, and drawings.

The idea is to create your ideal image to provide your mind with a clear picture of your heart's desires. Be sure to include a picture of yourself in the center of your treasure map! Spend a few minutes every day looking at your treasure map and meditating on the images. Be open to the manifestation of your goal, especially opportunities that appear in unexpected ways.

If you create a treasure map, you might want to journal about your experience. Have you had experiences of your imagination creating your reality? How might you engage your imagination to realize your dreams?

SUNDAY

When the soul wishes to experience something she throws an image of the experience out before her and enters into her own image.

—Meister Eckhart

MONDAY

The Possible's slow fuse is lit by the Imagination.

—Emily Dickinson

Tuesday

Imagination is more important than knowledge.

—Albert Einstein

Wednesday

Increase in imagination is always an increase in soul.

—Thomas Moore

THURSDAY

When we create something we always create it first in thought form.

—Shakti Gawain

FRIDAY

The world of reality has its limits; the world of imagination is boundless.

—Jean-Jacques Rousseau

Saturday

You are never given a dream without also being given the power to make it true.

—Richard Bach

Week 41

Rediscovering Your Creativity

Young children are wonderful, bold, risk-taking artists. Free from self-criticism, they paint purple trees and draw flowers with smiling faces. Watch children work with clay, and you'll see them make fanciful animals with six legs and three horns.

Something happens at an early age, though, and creativity gives way to conformity. It's tough for a creative spirit to survive without nurturing, and some people never again give their inner artist free reign.

It's never too late, however, to invite the artist within you to come out to play. The truth is, we all need to be artists in our lives. Creativity is an outward manifestation of your authentic self. Because you are unique, you create in ways like no one else. You don't have to paint, or draw, or do anything else traditionally considered as "art." What is important is that you do what makes your heart and spirit happy.

Look around you for clues to your self-expression. How have you decorated your home? What does your clothing say about you? Do you garden or arrange flowers? Perhaps you enjoy cooking or setting a beautiful table. Maybe you are known for making beautiful gifts or hosting memorable parties.

There are infinite ways of bringing your unique creativity to life, and much of the delight is in the exploration. Perhaps in reflecting upon your creativity you find yourself feeling vaguely dissatisfied, and out of touch with the artist within you.

Maybe you don't feel creative at all. Maybe you feel a bit scared. These are all natural feelings. It takes time for your inner artist to feel safe. Expressing yourself creatively can feel like an enormous risk. I assure you it is a worthwhile one. A wonderful companion in the journey is *The Artist's Way,* an inspiring guidebook by Julia Cameron.

This week, jot down ideas for bringing more creativity into your life. Start a file of images that intrigue you—clip pictures from design, clothing, gardening, and food magazines, and collect postcards and photos. Just for fun, take a trip to an art supply store and buy watercolor pencils, rubber stamps, colored pens, a drawing pad, and anything else that catches the fancy of your inner artist.

Sunday

Every child is an artist. The problem is how to remain an artist once he grows up.

—Pablo Picasso

Monday

To live a creative life, we must lose our fear of being wrong.

—Joseph Chilton Pearce

TUESDAY

To be surrounded by beautiful things has much influence upon the human creature: to make beautiful things has more.

—Charlotte Perkins Gilman

WEDNESDAY

When the creative urge seizes me—at least, such is my experience—one becomes creative in all directions at once.

—Henry Miller

Thursday

Creative minds have always been known to survive any kind of bad training.

—Anna Freud

Friday

Joy is but the sign that creative emotion is fulfilling its purpose.

—Charles Du Bos

SATURDAY

Odd how the creative power at once brings the whole universe to order.

—Virginia Woolf

Week 42

Finding Humor in Life

Cultivating a sense of humor is one of the surest ways of maintaining a joyful spirit. We often associate humor with fun and lightness, and yet, finding humor in what is difficult or painful helps to ease almost any situation. Far from being frivolous, humor can strengthen us and provide a resilience that helps us bounce back from difficulties.

Think of how you feel after a good laugh. Laughter relaxes your body, clears your mind, and uplifts your spirit. It actually strengthens your immune system and helps you stay healthy.

Most of all, laughter helps you keep life in perspective. It's easy to get overly serious about life—in fact, you were probably given that exact message at one time or another. "Be serious! This is no time for joking around!" If you took those messages to heart, your sense of humor may need some coaxing to come out to play. Fortunately, you have many tools at your disposal to rekindle your sense of humor.

You might start by checking out the comedy section in a video store. Comedies starring Meg Ryan, Kevin Kline, Woody Allen, or Steve Martin always make me laugh. I also enjoy writers who take a humorous slant on life, such as Anne Lamott, James Thurber, and Dave Barry.

My favorite kind of wit is that which finds the humor in everyday life. The commonplace becomes hilarious when magnified or viewed from a skewed, but humorous, perspective. Poking fun at ourselves and the situations in which we find ourselves can be immensely healing. There is a lot to be serious about in life, but there is also little that cannot be made lighter with a dose of humor.

This week, recall the last time you enjoyed a really good laugh. What do you find humorous? Would you like to bring more laughter into your life? Each day, try to find at least one thing that struck you as humorous. With a little practice, you'll develop a sharp eye for the humor in everyday life.

SUNDAY

The most thoroughly wasted of all days is that on which one has not laughed.

—Nicolas de Chamfort

MONDAY

I can imagine no more comfortable frame of mind for the conduct of life than a humorous resignation.

—William Somerset Maugham

TUESDAY

Humor brings insight and tolerance.

—AGNES REPPLIER

WEDNESDAY

Laughter is the sun that drives winter from the human face.

—VICTOR HUGO

Thursday

You can turn painful situations around through laughter. If you can find humor in anything...you can survive it.

—Bill Cosby

Friday

Humor is mankind's greatest blessing.

—Mark Twain

SATURDAY

Laughter is an instant vacation!

—Milton Berle

Week 43

The Art of Contentment

This morning I rose early, drank a cup of Earl Grey tea, wrote in my journal, went for a long walk with a close friend, and worked in my garden for an hour. It was an ordinary morning, almost identical to the way most of my days begin.

As I stood in the kitchen arranging flowers from my garden, I realized I felt deeply contented—a peaceful happiness filled my soul, and there was nothing I lacked. When I feel contented, I'm not searching, striving, or working at anything. I'm just being, and enjoying the pleasure of the moment.

I've found that contentment is very amenable to being nurtured. When I start to feel out-of-sorts, edgy, and my view of the world veers toward the negative, I try to realign myself with what brings me contentment. In fact, I usually plan my days so that each includes the ingredients that inspire contentment within me. These tend to be simple pleasures. A walk with a friend, relaxing in a beautiful spot outdoors, reading a wonderful novel, gardening, cooking, soaking in a bath, and browsing in an art gallery are a few of my favorite things to do. If I take time for these simple pleasures, my life seems richer and I am happier as a result.

Of course, the art of contentment also includes appreciating what we have right here in this moment. The more you cultivate appreciation and gratitude, the more contented you will feel. But it's not wrong to want more—to want to express your uniqueness, to please yourself, and to enjoy your life to the fullest.

This week, think about what it would take to feel gloriously satisfied. You might want to make a list of things that make you feel contented, from a morning shower with lavender soap to a cup of hot cocoa at night. Think of as many things as you can that bring you a warm glow of contentment. How many of these simple pleasures can you weave into your daily life? How might you arrange your day to nourish contentment in your soul?

Sunday

To affect the quality of the day, that is the highest of arts.

—Henry David Thoreau

Monday

Perhaps if one really knew when one was happy one would know the things that were necessary for one's life.

—Joanna Field

Tuesday

I have learned, in whatsoever state I am, therewith to be content.

—Saint. Paul

Wednesday

That it will never come again is what makes life so sweet.

—Emily Dickinson

THURSDAY

One's destination is never a place but rather a new way of looking at things.

—Henry Miller

FRIDAY

Write it on your heart that every day is the best day in the year.

—Ralph Waldo Emerson

Saturday

The amount of satisfaction you get from life depends largely on your own ingenuity, self-sufficiency, and resourcefulness. People who wait around for life to supply their satisfaction usually find boredom instead.

--William Menninger, M.D.

Week 44

Nurturing the Heart of Compassion

My dad is one of the most compassionate people I know. He's never studied philosophy or religion, but has an innate sense that we are all one, and lives from his heart, with a natural reverence for life. He fixes flat tires for strangers, makes household repairs for friends, cares for stray and injured animals, and is always willing to lend a helping hand, a sympathetic ear, or whatever else may be needed in the moment.

Most acts of compassion are just that simple. Compassion arises from the recognition of need in another being, the awareness of the commonality of our experience, and the desire to do what is possible to alleviate suffering.

It is painful, heart opening, and life transforming to truly understand, even for a moment, that we are all in this together. Compassion is not about feeling sorry for someone or something. It's the deep realization that none of us escape pain. The only way to make peace with this knowledge is to extend loving kindness toward ourselves and others.

As Jon Kabat-Zinn writes in his beautiful guide to living with awareness, *Wherever You Go There You Are,* "Being whole and simultaneously part of a larger whole, we can change the world simply by changing ourselves. If I become a center of love and kindness in this moment, then in a perhaps small but hardly insignificant way, the world now has a nucleus of love and kindness it lacked the moment before. This benefits me and it benefits others."

In practicing compassion, we must begin with ourselves. It's not possible to feel compassion for someone else if we don't grant ourselves the same kindness and understanding.

This week, reflect on compassion. Do you treat yourself with loving kindness? Journal about some ways in which you can be gentler with yourself. Imagine extending your compassion to others. In what ways can you express loving kindness in your daily life?

Sunday

Compassion is the natural response of the heart unclouded by the specious view that we are separate from one another.

—Sylvia Boorstein

Monday

If we could read the secret history of our enemies, we would find in each man's life a sorrow and a suffering enough to disarm all hostility.

—Henry Wadsworth Longfellow

Tuesday

Too often we underestimate the power of a touch, a smile, a kind word, a listening ear, an honest compliment, or the smallest act of caring, all of which have the potential to turn a life around.

—Leo Buscaglia

Wednesday

Life will bring you pain all by itself. Your responsibility is to create joy.

—Milton Erikson

Thursday

We resonate with one another's sorrows because we are interconnected.

—Jon Kabat-Zinn

Friday

We are all affecting the world every moment, whether we mean to or not. Our actions and states of mind matter, because we're so deeply interconnected with one another.

—Ram Dass

Saturday

My religion is kindness.

—The Dalai Lama

Week 45

The Spirit of Generosity

My friend Ann inspires me with her generosity. She works several hours a week in the garden of a friend who is ill, and made space in her home for a young mother and child struggling to piece their lives together. Not long ago, she transferred two weeks of her vacation time to a colleague who was undergoing chemotherapy.

Ann is not wealthy in the material sense, but she lives a rich life, full of friends and activities. She has made a conscious choice to work part-time so that she can pursue the things she loves to do, which include gardening, writing, and studying piano.

One reason Ann is able to give so generously to others is because she does a good job of also giving to herself.

There is a simple truth at the core of generosity—it's not possible to give away that which you do not possess, or that which you are not willing to give to yourself. When we are stingy with ourselves, we cannot help but be stingy with others. Even if you try to give, there will be strings attached, because there is the underlying fear that you are giving away something you do not really have to give.

Giving to yourself means not only providing for your basic needs for shelter, food, and clothing, but also giving generously to nourish your heart's desires. I find that when I give generously to myself, I then have the energy, resources, and enthusiam to give to others.

Many fears can come up around giving, including fears about not having enough, fears of being taken advantage of, or fears that people will start expecting too much. When we give from a place of fullness, there is less likelihood that these fears will control our generosity. Being grateful, and noticing all that we have in this moment, opens us to the awareness of abundance that is in our lives. This gratefulness, in turn, allows us to feel we have more than enough to give. "Gratitude creates a sense of fullness...and from this fullness, we feel moved to give...we give best from overflow," writes M. J. Ryan in her beautiful book, *Attitudes of Gratitude*.

Do you have impulses of generosity upon which you don't act? If so, what gets in the way? This week, reflect on how generous you feel in your life, and how often you act on your impulses to be generous. Consider that the greatest gifts we can offer are often not material—instead, they are the gifts of attention, a helping hand, a kind word, a loving gesture. As M. J. Ryan says, "When we live with a grateful heart, we will see endless opportunities to give. You will know what to do."

SUNDAY

Above all, generosity is an inward giving, a feeling state, a willingness to share your own being with the world.

—Jon Kabat-Zinn

MONDAY

The more you feel grateful, the stronger is the impulse toward giving.

—M. J. Ryan

Tuesday

I am only one, but still I am one. I cannot do everything, but still I can do something. I will not refuse to do the something I can do.

—Helen Keller

Wednesday

Big-heartedness is the most essential virtue on the spiritual journey.

—Matthew Fox

THURSDAY

If I can stop one heart from breaking, I shall not live in vain.
If I can ease one life the aching, or cool one pain,
or help one fainting robin into his nest again, I shall not live in vain.

—Emily Dickinson

FRIDAY

Each of us will one day be judged by our standard of life...not by our
standard of living; by our measure of giving...not by our measure of wealth,
by our simple goodness...not by our seeming greatness.

—William Arthur Ward

Saturday

*If you think you have given enough, think again.
There is always more to give and someone to give it to.*

—Norman Vincent Peale

Week 46

Connecting with Friends

I've made several significant geographic moves in my life, each time finding myself separated from friends by thousands of miles. I vowed to keep in touch with every move, but time and distance have a way of eroding even the best intentions. However, I'm finding it not so easy or desirable to consider another move in my life, and much of my hesitation has to do with not wanting to again leave friends behind.

It's easy to make acquaintances, but it's not so easy to make a true friend. Friendship takes time, trust, and shared experiences, and there's no shortcut. A true friendship encompasses shared hopes and dreams, confidences, difficult times as well as celebrations of life, joy and pain—and in the process, lives are woven together.

Friendships are like marriage in many ways. They take nurturing and care, but the rewards are great.

Knowing that you can share your deepest thoughts and truly reveal yourself to another is one of the soul-nurturing delights of a close friendship. I've found that a healthy friendship nourishes the emergence of the authentic self, and provides encouragement along the often emotionally challenging path of becoming whole.

It's not realistic to expect any one friend to meet all of your needs, just as it's not realistic or healthy to expect your life partner to meet all of your needs. What all of my close friends have in common, however, is the commitment to be authentic and a desire to live life to the fullest.

This week, take some time to remember—or write about—your close friends. What qualities attract you to those friends? Do your friendships nurture and support your authentic self? Think, too, of some people you are just getting to know. Are there opportunities for friendships in your relationships with them?

SUNDAY

Friendship is the inexpressible comfort of feeling safe with a person, having neither to weigh thoughts nor measure words.

—George Eliot

MONDAY

The only way to have a friend is to be one.

—Ralph Waldo Emerson

Tuesday

No one would choose a friendless existence on condition of having all the other things in the world.

—Aristotle

Wednesday

We are here to awaken from the illusion of our separateness.

—Thich Nhat Hanh

THURSDAY

If we would build on a sure foundation in friendship,
we must love friends for their sake rather than for our own.

—Charlotte Brontë

FRIDAY

Each friend represents a world in us, a world possibly not born until they arrive,
and it is only by this meeting that a new world is born.

—Anaïs Nin

Saturday

Wishing to be friends is quick work, but friendship is slow ripening fruit.

—Aristotle

Week 47

Rediscovering Love

Love is perhaps the most powerful of our desires, and yet it also seems to be the most elusive to fulfill. Most of us have experienced the intoxicating feeling of falling in love—we are immersed in our beloved, we see ourselves and everything around us in the glow of love, and our lives are infused with meaning. When the initial heady feeling dissipates—and it always does—we're likely to feel disillusioned, wondering where love went. Many times we begin the search for love anew, or perhaps we lose faith altogether in love, believing it to be unattainable.

Sometimes, leaving a relationship is the healthiest choice we can make, especially if we entered into the relationship without being conscious of who we truly are. Lacking that consciousness, it seems almost inevitable that our paths diverge irreconcilably along the way.

Many times, however, simply changing perspective can be all that is needed to rekindle love. Unconsciously, we often love conditionally, expecting our beloved to fulfill our needs and projecting onto him or her all that we desire for ourselves. This common romantic idea of love is continually reinforced through movies, books, and the media, and it takes looking at ourselves and our partners with honesty, compassion, and the wisdom of experience to begin to break free of this love-destroying misconception.

You leave little room for individuality within your relationship when you love someone conditionally. The most important thing you can do to nurture deep, passionate, and enduring love is to respect each other's individuality. Allow space within your relationship for expressing your authentic selves.

In his book *To Love and Be Loved*, Sam Keen suggests an exercise that I find helpful for rekindling and nurturing love. Focus on your partner, and describe him or her in the way you habitually see that person. Now, imagine you are seeing him or her for the first time, and create a new description, from this different viewpoint.

What do you notice about this person when you are not filtering your observations through your judgments? What happens to your feelings as you make this shift in consciousness?

This week, reflect on your experiences with love. Consider how satisfying your love relationships have been for you. What have you learned about yourself through these relationships?

If you are in a relationship now, how much freedom do you give yourself and your partner to express your authentic selves? What, if anything, would you like to change about the way you approach relationships?

Sunday

Love one another, but make no bond of love;
Let it rather be a moving sea between the shores of your souls.

—Kahlil Gibran

Monday

The seed of love must be eternally resown.

—Anne Morrow Lindbergh

Tuesday

On this earth there is no perfect love, only human love.

—Leo Buscaglia

Wednesday

Love is the child of freedom, never that of domination.

—Erich Fromm

Thursday

To truly love people, we must first be able to let them be—let them be who they are, not who we would like them to be.

—John Welwood

Friday

Love is not only something you feel. It is something you do.

—David Wilkerson

Saturday

I believe that we invite people into our lives, especially our partners, to be our teachers. The irony of this is that, having invited them to be our teachers, we then go kicking and screaming into the classroom!

—Patricia Love

Week 48

The Sanctuary of Home

Imagine a home that welcomes you when you walk through the doorway—a haven that restores your body, refreshes your mind, and brings peace and joy to your spirit. Perhaps this is how you feel about your home. If so, you know the deep satisfaction that comes from creating a nurturing place in which to live.

Making a home is one of the most important and sacred endeavors upon which you can embark. For far too many of us, though, home has taken a backseat to the pursuit of careers and outside activities.

Granted, there is much in life that calls for our attention. Without a nurturing home, however, there is no place for renewing your body, mind, and spirit. You need a place where you can retreat, and recoup your forces, before you return to the outside world.

Your home is an outward reflection of you. As such, it offers endless opportunities for creativity and for supporting the expression of your authentic self.

This week, take time to observe your home as though seeing it for the first time. Does the overall impression please you? Is it a home that offers comfort, beauty, and serenity? Do you feel a sense of well-being and pleasure when you come home? Is there one room, more than all the others, that seems like a true expression of your authentic self?

Experiment with visualizing your ideal home. What would it look like, and feel like, if it were a place that perfectly reflected your authentic self? As you imagine your ideal home in rich detail, journal about it. What color would you paint the walls, and what kind of artwork would you choose? What furniture would you select, and how would you arrange it? Visualize comfortable places in every room and imagine every detail, down to the towels, the bed linens, and the kitchen ware. How closely does your ideal home match the home you are living in now? What changes do you want to make to bring your ideal home into being?

SUNDAY

There is no place more delightful than home.

—Marcus Cicero

MONDAY

Where we love is home, home that our feet may leave, but not our hearts.

—Oliver Wendell Holmes, Sr.

Tuesday

We shape our dwellings, and afterwards our dwellings shape us.

—Sir Winston Churchill

Wednesday

A house is no home unless it contains food and fire for the mind as well as the body.

—Margaret Fuller

Thursday

He is happiest, be he king or peasant, who finds peace in his home.

—Johann Wolfgang von Goethe

Friday

Have nothing in your homes that you do not know to be useful and believe to be beautiful.

—William Morris

SATURDAY

The ordinary arts we practice every day at home are of more importance to the soul than their simplicity might suggest.

—Thomas Moore

Week 49

Enjoying Optimal Health

Over the course of almost three decades, I've experimented with many different health practices—including vegetarianism, jogging, juice fasts, meditation, and yoga—in my quest for optimal health and well-being. Some things suited me well. Yoga and meditation helped me to relax and made my body and mind feel good, and they continue to be an important part of my life.

I've given up strict vegetarianism, running long distances, and juice fasts, however. Even though I believed they were good for me, they didn't make me feel good. Jogging hurt my knees, and I never looked forward to it. Juice fasts drained my energy. And several years of following a strict vegetarian diet took a toll on my vitality.

It's taken me a long time to wake up to the fact that I can trust my body, and that if something I am doing doesn't make me feel good, then it's probably not right for me.

We are all individuals, with unique physical makeups. Obviously, we have much in common with each other: We all need healthful food, exercise, and rest. Within these areas of common ground, however, each of us has a great deal of latitude to discover what's right for us individually.

You can discover the optimal diet for your particular needs. You can find ways of exercising that work just right for your body. You can determine the amount of rest and relaxation that are ideal for you.

True, we are continually bombarded with an avalanche of nutrition, exercise, and lifestyle advice—and much of that advice is in conflict with what we may have heard before. But despite the onslaught of information and advice, it's important to recognize that no health expert can tell you exactly what's best for *your* body and well-being.

When I came to that realization, I began to discover my own ways of enjoying good health. I learned that although I didn't like running, I loved long, brisk walks—especially with friends. So that's what I do these days. Aerobics classes bored me, but now I've discovered a passion for dance. As far as diet goes, I've learned to eat what my body craves, not according to the strictures of someone else's dietary philosophy, and my diet has become satisfying and well-rounded as well as healthful.

Discovering what's exactly right for you takes time, experimentation, and the willingness to listen to your body. This week, reflect on how you might listen more carefully to your body's needs. What changes would you like to make, and how can you make those changes enjoyable and just right for you?

SUNDAY

*Show your body how much you appreciate and respect it.
You will glow with strength and health.*

—Shakti Gawain

MONDAY

The first wealth is health.

—Ralph Waldo Emerson

Tuesday

God bless the roots! Body and soul are one.

—Theodore Roethke

Wednesday

Our bodies are our allies, and they will always point us in the direction we need to go next.

—Christiane Northrup, M.D.

Thursday

If you are willing to allow the energy of the universe to move through you by trusting and following your intuition, you will increase your sense of aliveness and your body will reflect this with increasing health, beauty, and vitality.

—Shakti Gawain

Friday

Many people understand the value of preventive maintenance in caring for their cars. It is strange that more of us do not apply the same concept to our bodies, which are infinitely more valuable.

—Andrew Weil, M.D.

SATURDAY

Every day in every way, I am getting better and better.

—Emile Coué

Week 50

The Restorative Power of Relaxation

Not long ago, I spent a full day at a nearby lake, floating in the crystal clear turquoise water, walking leisurely around the pine-scented trail, and relaxing on the rocky beach beneath the trees. For a while, I simply watched the water lapping at the shore.

That was a day of pure relaxation—a time-out from the busyness of everyday life, with all of its intricacies and projects and deadlines. There were plenty of things calling for my attention at home and at work, but that day of relaxation took precedence over everything else.

I've found that I can't wait until everything is completed to take time out for relaxation. We have to deliberately set aside time to relax, or we'll never get around to it.

Relaxation is like stepping off a merry-go-round. Life keeps on going, and it's all too easy to get caught in the whirling round of activities and to allow them to dictate our lives. There is no end to the projects and tasks and commitments.

We can simplify and decide to not overcommit ourselves, but even with a pared-down life, we still need time for pure relaxation. We need time away from everything routine—a vacation for the body, mind, and spirit.

Taking time out in this way is deeply restorative. Even an hour in the midst of a busy day can be wonderfully refreshing. Perhaps, in addition to taking time on the weekends for relaxation, you can go to a nearby park during the week just to sit for a while. You'll find this brief timeout from your daily routine brings much needed balance to your life.

During the week ahead, make a few notes about the time you allow yourself for relaxation. How do you feel when you relax? What are your favorite ways to take a break?

Can you discover some moments, amid the busyness of daily life, when it's possible to get away—even if it's just for a few minutes?

SUNDAY

Life gives us scant time for being these days, unless we seize it on purpose.

—Jon Kabat-Zinn

MONDAY

*Every now and then go away, have a little relaxation,
for when you come back to your work your judgment will be surer.*

—Leonardo da Vinci

TUESDAY

*A day out-of-doors, someone I loved to talk with,
a good book and some simple food and music—that would be rest.*

—ELEANOR ROOSEVELT

WEDNESDAY

*You will find that deep place of silence right in your room, your garden,
or even your bathtub.*

—ELISABETH KÜBLER-ROSS, M.D.

Thursday

*Yet it is in our idleness, in our dreams,
that the submerged truth sometimes comes to the top.*

—Virginia Woolf

Friday

*When our minds and bodies are deeply relaxed and centered . . .
we have a chance to listen on a deeper level. We become receptive
and open to our creative imagination and intuition.*

—Shakti Gawain

SATURDAY

The secret of life is balance, and the absence of balance is life's destruction.

—Hazrat Inayat Khan

Week 51

Cultivating Peace

Peace. Just the word itself elicits a feeling of calm, a sense of all being right with the world. Peace restores physical well-being, eases the mind, and nourishes the soul. When we are at peace, time seems to slow down, and life becomes effortless.

What helps you to feel peaceful? Take a moment to reflect, allowing images and feelings to arise. Notice how you feel when you reflect on peaceful moments. When was the last time you felt a deep sense of peace? Do you find peace elusive?

Peace often seems like a gift of grace, arising spontaneously and then just as quickly dissipating. You can learn to cultivate peace, how-ever, in much the same way you would cultivate a garden. The more attention you pay to preparing the soil, providing nutrients, and nurturing the plants, the more abundant your harvest will be. It's the same with peace. When you allow time for quiet solitude and self-reflection, you are inviting peace (preparing the soil) by calming your body, mind, and spirit.

You can also provide inspiration for peace—that is, food for your soul. The inspiration can come in the form of journaling, meditating, praying, reading inspirational books, listening to meditative music, or taking a quiet walk. You can nurture feelings of peace and help them to grow stronger by cultivating gratitude, practicing forgiveness of yourself and others, and living in alignment with your authentic self.

It is possible to live peacefully, even in the midst of a busy and complex life. Other than fleeting moments, however, peace isn't likely to be manifested unless you seek it with conscious intention and devote some part of your awareness to it.

Take time this week to pay attention to moments of peace that arise spontaneously. Notice how your perspective of life is transformed when you feel at peace. What can you do to nourish peace in your life?

Sunday

Nothing can bring you peace but yourself.

—Ralph Waldo Emerson

Monday

Peace is not a passive but an active condition.

—Mary Roberts Rinehart

Tuesday

It isn't enough to talk about peace. One must believe in it. And it isn't enough to believe in it. One must work at it.

—Eleanor Roosevelt

Wednesday

During each moment that we are aware of something peaceful and beautiful, we water seeds of peace and beauty in us.

—Thich Nhat Hanh

THURSDAY

Whatever peace I know rests in the natural world,
in feeling myself a part of it, even in a small way.

—May Sarton

FRIDAY

Peace is not won by those who fiercely guard their differences but by
those who with open minds and hearts seek out connections.

—Katherine Paterson

Saturday

If there is to be any peace it will come through being, not having.

—Henry Miller

Week 52

The Essence of Spirituality

As you follow the path of your heart's desires, you are led to the core of your being, and to the unique expression of your authentic self. There can be no more sacred work than that of becoming all that we are meant to be. By paying attention to the details of life, all of life is experienced as sacred.

"Too commonly, some things are thought of as spiritual while others are excluded," writes Jon Kabat-Zinn in *Wherever You Go There You Are*, his inspiring guide to mindfulness in everyday life. "Ultimately, spiritual simply means experiencing wholeness and interconnectedness directly. If you see in this way, then everything becomes spiritual in its deepest sense."

Washing the dishes, meditating, cooking dinner, taking out the trash, reading, walking in the woods, talking with a friend . . . everything is spiritual when we are awake in the moment. I have found that the practice of awakening to the present moment is what gives my life meaning—a center to which I can return again and again. It is a life-long practice. It is a practice of remembering, forgetting, remembering, forgetting, and remembering yet again.

The quest for the answer to the meaning of life is an ancient one, a common thread that ties together all of the peoples of the world from the beginning of time. It is, ultimately, a question that we must answer for ourselves. You will know when you encounter what is true for you—it will resonate deep within your being, nourish your soul, and give meaning and purpose to your existence.

There are many paths to truth, or what we may call spirit. All truth involves looking deeply within ourselves, recognizing what is good and endeavoring to live as best we can, being honest, loving ourselves and each other, and forgiving ourselves and each other for being human and fallible.

Appreciating the gifts of daily life opens our hearts to spirit. Above all, doing our best to recognize and fully live our heart's desires brings us to the place where spirit burns brightly within us and illuminates all that we do.

This week, reflect on what spirituality means to you. What kind of spiritual upbringing did you have? Have your ideas of spirituality changed over time? What do you do now, every day, to nurture spirit in your life?

Sunday

The soul should always stand ajar, ready to welcome the ecstatic experience.

—Emily Dickinson

Monday

Any time we are fully present in the moment we are meditating.

—Joan Borysenko

Tuesday

Mindfulness practice means that we commit fully in each moment to being present. There is no 'performance.' There is just this moment.

—Jon Kabat-Zinn

Wednesday

Our own life is the instrument with which we experiment with truth.

—Thich Nhat Hanh

Thursday

To keep a lamp burning we have to keep putting oil in it.

—Mother Teresa

Friday

I long to accomplish a great and noble task, but it is my chief duty to accomplish small tasks as if they were great and noble.

—Helen Keller

Saturday

What matters is how we live. That is why it is so important to ask this question of ourselves: "Am I living my path fully, do I live without regret?"

—Jack Kornfield

About the Author

Laurel Vuković, M.S.W., has worked in the field of natural healing for two decades as a psychotherapist, herbalist, teacher, and writer. Since 1992, she has been a columnist and contributing editor for Natural Health magazine and is the author of *14-Day Herbal Cleansing* and *Herbal Healing Secrets for Women* (both from Prentice Hall Press). She has kept a journal for more than 20 years as a path to living an authentic life.